THE FORMATIONAL POWER OF WORSHIP

Leading Your Community with Intention

TIMOTHY BROOKS

THE FOUNDRY
PUBLISHING

Copyright © 2020 by Timothy Brooks
The Foundry Publishing
PO Box 419527
Kansas City, MO 64141
thefoundrypublishing.com

ISBN 978-0-8341-3788-2

All rights reserved. No part of this publication may be reproduced, stored in a retrieval system, or transmitted in any form or by any means—for example, electronic, photocopy, recording—without the prior written permission of the publisher. The only exception is brief quotations in printed reviews.

Cover design: Mike Williams
Interior design: Sharon Page

Unless otherwise indicated, all Scripture quotations are from the Holy Bible, New International Version® (NIV®). Copyright © 1973, 1978, 1984, 2011 by Biblica, Inc.™ Used by permission of Zondervan. All rights reserved worldwide. www.zondervan.com. The "NIV" and "New International Version" are trademarks registered in the United States Patent and Trademark Office by Biblica, Inc.™

The following version of Scripture is in the public domain:

The King James Version (KJV)

The following copyrighted versions of Scripture are used by permission:

The Holy Bible, English Standard Version® (ESV®). Copyright © 2001 by Crossway Bibles, a publishing ministry of Good News Publishers. All rights reserved.

The Expanded Bible (EXB). Copyright © 2011 by Thomas Nelson. Used by permission. All rights reserved.

Library of Congress Cataloging-in-Publication Data

Names: Brooks, Timothy, 1981- author.
Title: The formational power of worship : leading your community with intention / Timothy Brooks.
Description: Kansas City, MO : The Foundry Publishing, 2020. | Includes bibliographical references. |
Summary: "This book invites you to begin to examine the different elements of worship, exploring how they can better become formational moments in the life of the church"— Provided by publisher.
Identifiers: LCCN 2020016613 (print) | LCCN 2020016614 (ebook) | ISBN 9780834137882 (paperback) | ISBN 9780834137899 (ebook)
Subjects: LCSH: Worship.
Classification: LCC BV10.3 .B76 2020 (print) | LCC BV10.3 (ebook) | DDC 264—dc23
LC record available at https://lccn.loc.gov/2020016613
LC ebook record available at https://lccn.loc.gov/2020016614

The Internet addresses, email addresses, and phone numbers in this book are accurate at the time of publication. They are provided as a resource. The Foundry Publishing does not endorse them or vouch for their content or permanence.

To my dearly beloved and missed mother, Mary L. Brooks (1955–2019). As my mom, you taught me how to worship. In death, your practice of glorifying God has been perfected in glory as your faith has become sight. This book would never have been conceived without your witness. May God be glorified on earth as he is in heaven by you and the great cloud of witnesses you have joined.

Contents

● ● ●

Foreword	7
Introduction	11
1. The Power of Subconscious Formation	17
2. Planning with Intention	25
3. Call to Worship	33
4. Singing	39
5. Reading Scripture	51
6. Prayer	63
7. Receiving the Offering	71
8. Greeting Time	85
9. Sermon	97
10. Response	113
11. Sacrament	119
12. Benediction	135
Afterword	151
Bibliography	159

Foreword

• • •

"We shape our buildings and afterwards our buildings shape us." In 1943, faced with the prospect of rebuilding the British House of Commons chamber following its destruction by bombing during World War II, Winston Churchill offered this observation on the formative power of architecture—how we build and organize space.[1]

Nearly twenty-five years later, Father John Culkin, SJ, writing about his friend and mentor, media theorist Marshall McLuhan, applied this concept to technology: "We shape our tools and thereafter they shape us."[2] Indeed, as our tools and devices extend our bodies and our human capacities, they not only reflect our desires and intentions but serve to form our very desires and intentions as well. We can see this in everything from our automobiles to our iPhones to language itself.

---

1. "Churchill and the Commons Chamber," UK Parliament, accessed March 26, 2020, https://www.parliament.uk/about/living-heritage/building/palace/architecture/palacestructure/churchill/.

2. John Culkin, "A Schoolman's Guide to Marshall McLuhan," *Saturday Review*, March 1967, 70.

Similarly, *the shape of our worship shapes us*. Worship, which brings together bodies in particular spaces, is in a sense a technology (Gk., *technē*: "art," "craft," "discipline") that expresses and reflects the human desire to commune with God and one another and simultaneously creates the conditions under which a gathered people "offer [their] bodies as a living sacrifice" (Rom. 12:1) and are thereby made into the body of Christ called church.

Tim Brooks is a pastor-theologian who understands the identity-shaping influence of both Christian worship and secular culture. He has thought long and hard about the relationship between spiritual and cultural formation, not far off in the ivory towers of the academy but up close in the parish, working day in and day out with the people who together are the "living stones . . . being built into a spiritual house to be a holy priesthood, offering spiritual sacrifices acceptable to God through Jesus Christ" (1 Pet. 2:5). Tim understands that worship, like culture, can just as easily malform and deform as transform and reform us, but what it cannot do is *not form* us. For good or ill, we cannot help but leave differently than we came in.

Too often, the formational power of worship is eclipsed by a utilitarian approach that is concerned more with relevance and results than with a renovation of the heart (to borrow a phrase from Dallas Willard[3]), the long game of cultivating holy habits through consistent, faithful personal and corporate practices. Shortsighted pragmatism may be attractive, but it perpetuates a consumer mindset that easily and inevitably spills over into worship. When the broader culture constantly tells us that the customer is king and that our individual happiness and fulfillment is the main

---

3. See Dallas Willard, *Renovation of the Heart: Putting on the Character of Christ* (Colorado Springs: NavPress, 2002).

thing, it is no surprise that we enter into worship postured less like Jesus—ready to be taken, blessed, broken, and given for the life of the world—and more like the judges on TV talent shows, scorecards at the ready.

And so it matters how we worship—what we do in worship, our words, our actions, our postures, our spaces and symbols. And it also matters how we engage and integrate culture into worship, because the images, narratives, symbols, and rituals in which we are immersed outside of the worship hour are also forming us continuously. Pastor Tim's belief (and mine, too) is that we need not fear the formative power of secular culture. God can and will use all of it. We can be confident that, through faithful, intentional worship practices, God is transforming us ever more deeply in Christlikeness and preparing us to be sent out into the world empowered by the Holy Spirit to "show forth your praise, not only with our lips, but in our lives, by giving up our selves to your service, and by walking before you in holiness and righteousness all our days."[4]

Rev. Brannon Hancock, PhD
Wesley Seminary

---

[4]. "The General Thanksgiving," *Book of Common Prayer* (New York: Church Hymnal Corporation, 1979), 101.

Introduction

• • •

I can remember my first Sunday as lead pastor as if it were yesterday. I had just graduated seminary with high honors, I had led a growing teen group, and I had served as a guest preacher numerous times. I was ready. I had been ruminating over my first sermon for weeks before taking the pulpit—my pulpit—for the first time. I wrote a manuscript with nuanced narratives, tight transitions, enlightening exegesis, and tremendous theology. I was prepared, cocky, and excited. I walked to the pulpit and read my entire sermon.

When finished, confident that I had contributed to the spiritual lives of these beautiful people—my flock—I looked up and realized I had nothing else planned. We were done because I was done. I do not recall my exact words to the congregation, but I told them it was time to go home.

Before I left, two laypeople spoke to me: one on reading sermon manuscripts (bad) and another on abrupt endings to worship services (also, bad). I wanted to respond, to point to my seminary experience with my impeccable GPA, but something deep within me knew they were right. As pastor, I was responsible for leading the people of God; I was charged with shepherding them into meaningful worship. What I had just done was to exhibit a public act of nerves and ego. Since that first day as pastor, I have been thinking about worship that is meaningful, that engages both heart and mind so that we can be shaped into disciples of a Jewish peasant who was crucified, dead, and buried, yet resurrected to glory.

The book of Revelation gives one of the best glimpses of properly ordered worship. Worship is where we publicly practice our longing for a kingdom yet to come in its fullness. This kingdom has been revealed in Christ, and John is allowed to see this worship. Seated at the center of heaven is a slaughtered Lamb on a throne. Elders and angels encircle the throne, completely fixated on the slaughtered Lamb. They sing songs of praise rooted in a faith that the Lamb has been and will be victorious. Orienting themselves in praise around the enthroned, slaughtered lamb becomes their identity.

The seven churches to which we are introduced in the second and third chapters of Revelation are also invited to orient their communal life and personal identities around this enthroned, slaughtered Lamb. Pastors of churches in the twenty-first century, similarly, are invited to imagine how we can orient our people around the slaughtered Lamb so that our worship time together invites our people to depart—or scatter—while imagining how they will remain oriented toward the slaughtered Lamb, following the Lamb wherever it goes.

Christians, the people of God called to orient our lives around Christ, have not always been great at reflecting Christ. Even in our acts of worship, we have sometimes looked more like the warring pagans of the world than like the Prince of Peace. The worship wars of the late 1990s and early 2000s were an extreme example of this. Drums or no drums? Guitars or organs? Praise teams or choirs? Liturgy or spontaneity? These arguments seem silly now, but they were intense and treated as vital during the war.

When war ends, reconstruction is messy. There is ravaged landscape, displaced people, opportunists, blame, political arguments, and loss of the way things were. Reconstruction is an ugly period in the history of the United States of America, and seeds sown in the aftermath of the Civil War remain strewn about 150 years later.

Harpers Ferry is a strategic piece of land in eastern West Virginia that changed hands a staggering eight times during the Civil War. Harpers Ferry was important, however, before the Civil War began. In 1859, abolitionist John Brown raided the federal armory at Harpers Ferry in order to arm slaves to incite a rebellion. Brown captured the armory, but he was caught within thirty-six hours, tried for murder, and hanged for his actions.

This escalated tension between the North and South helped lead to the secession of the Southern states just over one year later. The Civil War remains the bloodiest, most personal war the United States has fought. The stench of this "brother versus brother" war still wafts over the country today.

War leads to breaks in relationships, suspicion of others, and the destruction of innocents. The worship wars have led to the same in the church. Suspicion remains between generations. Angry letters written over song selections to song leaders, suspicions against sacramental worship, church plants formed over worship-style conflicts, and many more painful accounts of this era of worship reconstruction are now a part of our story.

The worship wars may be over, but the suspicion and anger remain.

The good news is that beauty can emerge from reconstruction, as it has on that hotly contested piece of land during the Civil

War, Harpers Ferry. At the end of the Civil War, the town of Harpers Ferry was in ruins. With little hope and little life in the town, a group of Freewill Baptists took over the house of a former armory paymaster—the same armory that John Brown seized.

The Baptists utilized the house to begin a primary school for freed African Americans in 1865. By 1867, the school had transformed into Storer College, a school that would be a continuous training ground for African American teachers until *Brown v. Board of Education* in 1955. Amid reconstruction in a famous war-ravaged place, a vision for the future was birthed and nurtured.

I suspect we are in a similar place in the church now. After fighting for decades over worship questions of *what* and *how*, perhaps we can turn to questions of *why*. Why do we sing in worship? Why do some churches pass the peace or have a greeting time? Why are sermons a part of worship? Answering *why* questions may help us understand what Christian worship is shaping us to be.

Simon Sinek, a noted leadership and business guru, observes in a famous *TED Talk*[1] that Apple is beating companies such as Dell because it is answering questions of *why* rather than *what*. Apple's attention not only on what it designs but also on why its products can enhance your life has given Apple an advantage over its equally qualified competitors.

Imagine preparing the Sunday morning service with the first driving question being not *what* but *why*. Imagine thinking about the formational power of each liturgical element. The important question is not "How many songs should we sing?" but "Why do

---

1. The lecture can be viewed in its entirety at Simon Sinek, "Start with Why—How Great Leaders Inspire Action," *TED Talk*, filmed September 28, 2009, YouTube video, 18:01, https://www.youtube.com/watch?v=u4ZoJKF_VuA.

we sing?" The question is not "Should we have an altar call?" but "Why have an altar call?"

This book will take you on a journey of *why*. Why do churches have calls to worship? Why do we sing, greet, read Scripture, pray together, preach sermons, serve the sacraments, and offer benedictions? In answering why these are done, you will be able to lead worship with intention, helping the people who gather for worship to be formed as the distinctly Christian people God is calling them to be. The Christian formation of persons into the holy people of God can begin in worship. As a local church leader, your job is to facilitate public gatherings of worship through which the church is called to be fully Christian. May this journey be a time of recalling the kingdom to which we are called and of recalling how we can invite our people to experience that kingdom for the sake of their formation into it. May our people leave the worship gathering formed to be citizens of the kingdom, living out kingdom principles in this world.

Note: This book is meant to encourage church leaders, musicians, ministry students, and pastors to come together and rethink issues of *why* around worship planning. Worship services are important formational moments in the life of the church. They are too important to use designations such as "contemporary" or "traditional"; "liturgical" or "charismatic." Some aspects of all of those styles can and should be present. But more is happening than what is implied by those designations. Let's journey through the possibilities together.

ONE
The Power of Subconscious Formation

• • •

Almost every parent has had to stop a curious child from touching a hot stove. As parents, we want our children to believe that touching the red coils or the burner's blue flame will lead to immense pain and horrific injury.

How do we go from curious child to careful adult? It is not simply by heeding parental warnings. Our parents share loads of information with us (especially from the ages of twelve to twenty) that we cast aside, confident we know better. No, we do not touch the hot stove, because we learned from a terrible experience or repeated warnings.

But what is amazing is that we do not need to decide whether or not to touch the red coils every time we see them. Our understanding of red coils becomes instinctual. When we see a hot stove, we react because we know without further thought that the heat is at a dangerous level.

How many times a day do we stop and think about what we are seeing and doing? Some, for sure, but much more often we react to our environment out of instinctual conditioning. There are many times that I leave my office, walk to my car, turn the key in the ignition, drive home, and wonder how I got there safely, even though my mind was elsewhere the whole time. There is something about what we know that becomes so embodied because of practice that we no longer need to actively think about what we are doing to do it well. We eventually no longer think—we just are. We grow up and do not need to be reminded constantly of what is dangerous. We transform, instead, into teachers because we have come to embody the lessons of how to behave safely. Safety is no longer a matter of the intellect or cognitive decision-making; it is who we are.

The philosophical word "habitus" describes acting out what we know deep within ourselves. Pierre Bourdieu, the French sociologist and philosopher, defines "habitus" as an "embodied history, internalized as a second nature and so forgotten as history."[1] Drawing from Bourdieu, James K. A. Smith, a contemporary philosophy professor at Calvin College, takes this idea of habitus and expands it. Smith points to the formation of a soldier as a colloquial example: A farm boy, he notes, joins the military, not because it makes sense based on the evidence, but because he has practiced patriotism his entire life. He has come to recognize its symbols as meaningful and decides it is worth giving his life to it. This is a decision formed out of one's habitus.[2]

---

1. See Mary Clark Moschella, *Ethnography as a Pastoral Practice: An Introduction* (Cleveland: Pilgrim Press, 2008), 52.
2. James K. A. Smith, *Desiring the Kingdom: Worship, Worldview, and Cultural Formation*, Cultural Liturgies, vol. 1 (Grand Rapids: Baker Academic, 2009), 103-11.

Once in the military, the habitus is transformed through practice. Boot camp is liturgical; a new kind of person is made through a specific set of prescribed acts. It takes practice to become a soldier. It takes practice to become a Christian as well. And it is in the seemingly mundane acts of worship that Christians are most strongly and properly formed—that is, in their being rather than solely in their thinking or believing. It takes practice, symbols, liturgies, and narratives regularly forming us at the subconscious level to change the fundamental way we engage with our world.

Maurice Merleau-Ponty speaks of what the body "knows," and this he calls perception. He says that we do not abstractly think our way through the world, but we are also not passive victims of impressions, controlled by instinctual reflexes. Our bodies are the vehicles of our being in the world, and our bodies carry with them an embodied knowledge.[3] You may also think of it as muscle memory. Our bodies do what they know to be true.

Smith tells the story of engaging Wendell Berry's book *Bringing It to the Table*. The book is about farming, eating, and stewardship. Smith seems to be assenting to the theses of Berry's work. When he is finished reading, he sets the book down and remembers that he is eating in a food court at Costco. This scene is precisely the context that Berry is attempting to challenge: food that is full of preservatives, mass-produced, shipped great distances, and so on. Smith argues that his mindless trip to Costco—and the habitus that undergirds this trip—overrides his intellectual assent to Berry's work.[4]

---

3. James K. A. Smith. *Imagining the Kingdom: How Worship Works*, Cultural Liturgies, vol. 2. (Grand Rapids: Baker Academic, 2013), 45.

4. Ibid., 8-10.

As Christians, we are interested in the way the Holy Spirit—whom we affirm as formational—affects the practices of our body. How do we as Christians allow ourselves to be formed so that our way of life is inscribed in our "habit body"? Or how can we intentionally allow the Spirit to orient our life in the world?[5]

This practicing of the body was teased out in a study of rats in the early 1990s at the Massachusetts Institute of Technology (MIT). A rat was placed in a T-shaped box, behind a wall at the bottom of the T. The wall was opened, and the rat was freed to roam. It would mindlessly stroll up the T, seeming to meander toward nothing. On the left side of the capital T would be a piece of chocolate. The first few times the rat would show immense brain activity but would not necessarily move toward the chocolate. Many times the rat would be released, and it would turn right, toward nothing. The more times the same rat would be released into the T, the less brain activity it would show and the more quickly the rat would move toward the chocolate.

Eventually, after a few days of learning the routine, the rat knew the situation. The door would open, and there was less evidence that the smelling or processing parts of the brain were firing. The rat simply heard the door open and made its way to where the chocolate was.[6] Eventually, it became a habit for the rat to hear the door open and go to the chocolate. It was written in its habitus.

The average church member probably does not consider that his or her habitus is being formed by worship. Attendance at worship services has often been described as "duty" and "obligation" rather than as formation. But what if more than "putting in time,"

---

5. Ibid., 45.
6. See Charles Duhigg, *The Power of Habit: Why We Do What We Do in Life and Business* (New York: Random House Trade Paperbacks, 2014), 14-16.

we begin to see our gathering for worship as a way of participating in the activities of heaven on earth that form us to be people of heaven on earth? We may feel some days that we are going through the motions, but that is okay. Our minds and bodies are being formed into knowing the ways of the kingdom. We move from thinking about how to act or be, to having an embodied reaction to God's presence in our gatherings.

Augustine of Hippo addressed this in terms of the city of God, as opposed to the earthly city. People focused on the earthly city immerse themselves in the pleasures and cares of this world. The city of God, however, is marked by people who see themselves in this world as citizens of the heavenly realm. They forgo earthly pleasures to dedicate themselves to the world that is to come.

But do we know how to do this? We gather as the people of God to worship, not only experiencing the glory of God but also practicing heaven together. We learn about heaven, or, perhaps better stated, the kingdom of God. In gathering to worship, we learn who we are and who we are becoming in Christ through the in-breaking of the Spirit in gathered worship. We practice heavenly worship, gathered with the saints, angels, and elders in heaven, as described in Revelation 4:

> In the center, around the throne, were four living creatures, and they were covered with eyes, in front and in back. The first living creature was like a lion, the second was like an ox, the third had a face like a man, the fourth was like a flying eagle. Each of the four living creatures had six wings and was covered with eyes all around, even under its wings. Day and night they never stop saying:
>
> > "'Holy, holy, holy
> > is the Lord God Almighty,'
> > who was, and is, and is to come."

Whenever the living creatures give glory, honor and thanks to him who sits on the throne and who lives for ever and ever, the twenty-four elders fall down before him who sits on the throne and worship him who lives for ever and ever. They lay their crowns before the throne and say:

"You are worthy, our Lord and God,
> to receive glory and honor and power,
for you created all things,
> > and by your will they were created
> > and have their being." (Vv. 6-11)

When we worship, we do not just sing to a God who is present; we sing with the heavens to a God who is present both in creation and in the coming New Jerusalem—the new creation. Therefore, we are practicing citizenship in heaven. Our worship is not simply praising God but practicing the very reality of who God is drawing us to be: the holy people of God. Worship forms us into our destiny.

I have started running. Growing up, I was an offensive lineman and baseball player. Neither demanded that I had to be in great shape. If I am honest, I was always out of shape. When sports ended and I went to college, I changed from overweight to obese. Meanwhile, I could not understand why anyone would purposely run for distance. The irony was as thick as my waistline.

During my seminary years, my father passed away from cancer. I wondered, privately, if his weight contributed to his cancer or inability to defeat cancer. This was, in retrospect, probably unfair, but grief invites the brain to wander. There was no medical evidence or doctor that suggested this; I simply wondered. While mourning my fifty-three-year-old father's passing, I decided I needed to live healthier.

Now I'm not trying to sound like Forrest Gump, but I started running.

I would run one mile, three times a week. I was pleased to see I was getting better at the discipline of running, and I was shedding weight too. I added dieting, and I lost a ton of weight. Running became easier, so I began playing soccer. The more soccer I played, the more I ran. The more I ran, the healthier I became. The healthier I became, the more competitive were the races I ran.

To this point, I have run five-kilometer, ten-kilometer, and ten-mile races. I never win, nor am I ever close to winning. But something strange has happened in the last decade: I became a runner. I am a runner. Running is not something I do; it is who I have become.

Similarly, worship is not something we do—not an obligation, not an appointment, not an entertainment venue. Worship is about who we are becoming. When we subject ourselves to the liturgy of the church, we invite Christ to be formed in us through the work we do as the people of God.

Alternately, skipping church becomes problematic because there is a world, economy, pop musician, actress, op-ed writer, newscaster, podcast host, or athlete more than willing to articulate who we should be. If worship can shape us, so can the unlimited activities our connected world offers us.

Much is at stake in whether or not we worship regularly. Our calendars are surely moral documents, testifying to the world what really matters to us. But more than that, we can quickly find our loves and lives being shaped by influences different from that of dwelling in the presence of God with other believers.

Moving forward, this book is going to walk through typical movements of worship. We will journey through seemingly mundane acts of worship (offering, greeting, etc.) in order to explore the kind of person we are invited to be as a result of our attending to the worship of God. As we make this journey, let us invite God to open our eyes to the value of mundane acts, that they may shape us to be citizens of a heavenly kingdom while inhabiting this world.

TWO
Planning with Intention

• • •

There are contrasting axioms I have heard all my life in church while evaluating worship services: the first is that you "shouldn't overplan a service or else you may miss the presence of the Spirit and what the Spirit is asking you to do." The other is that "it is beautiful when the special song, testimony, or presentation lined up perfectly with the sermon." In such moments, people will sometimes declare that it was "as if God knew what God was doing by prompting the singer, preacher, reader [all separately]."

Why can't God prompt in a planning session? Why can't God inspire months before a service? There has been a tendency in evangelical Protestant circles to feel most assured of the nearness of the Spirit when no one knows what is coming next in a service, but everything fits together well in the end.

Can we confess that what we like is the fitting together well, the cohesive narrative of a flowing worship service? We can achieve this weekly by working together in planning sessions empowered by prayer, conjoined with discernment, and equipped with church calendars to orchestrate a Spirit-ordained and coherent service well before we arrive in worship. The same Spirit we think brings together different moments in a service can also work in a planning session weeks or months in advance.

For as much pomp and circumstance that we ascribe the uncommunicated occurrences of cohesion, we worship planners also have moments when we are baffled by the lectionary text the week after an atrocity or the timely direction a sermon series, planned months ago, turns perfectly the week a much-loved church member dies.

I am convinced that God is at work in the details. God is at work in the planning. God provides us, through prayerful discernment, a vision for how a worship service will flow toward narrative cohesion.

But what are we planning for? The service should not serve the planner's ego so that people compliment it as a "nice service" as they shake the pastor's hand before leaving. The plan should not focus solely on seekers, and the plan should not focus solely on those saved. The plan of a worship service should point people toward discipleship in Christ. That pointing can be done for a seeker, a convert, a person of nominal faith, or a faithful disciple. A well-done worship service should attend to the five senses of the full gathering, speaking to the longings of their habitus, pointing those longings in the direction of Christ so that their habitus would be formed to yearn for Christ. As worship gatherings are conducted, we should consider how smell, sight, hearing, touch, and taste could all be engaged so that we are using the full experience of human life to touch the habitus of our people.

When planning, we—pastors, worship leaders, musicians, prayers, readers, leaders—should think well beyond *what*. It is important to ask, What is the theme? What is the way to tie the theme together? Those are important questions. More difficult, and important, is to ask, Why do we do what we do? What are we hoping, in our planning, will happen to, for, and through our congregants? We should be forming the habitus of our people.

James K. A. Smith argues convincingly in his book *Desiring the Kingdom* that all of life is liturgical. Our people are subjected to all manner of cultural liturgies. Heading to the mall, participating in a sporting event, being patriotic—all have learned patterns and bodily responses that indicate our devotion and in turn shape our innermost responses to the activities. Our very precognitive behavior is shaped by the way cultural liturgies shape our longings and desires.

The church would do well to remember that it has a liturgical life as well. It's liturgical acts—singing, giving, passing the peace, hearing sermons, coming to the Table of our Lord—are not ends in themselves but activities that shape how we live and who we will be.

Our worship services should be formational at our innermost level. Our gathering in worship should be triggering our longings for who we want to be so that they mirror God's longing of who we ought to be.

The church has sensed for years that our desires can be formed by what we do. While I grew up, the major values the church thrust upon me ensured that I did not drink alcohol, use profanity, or have premarital sex. To avoid any of those activities, it was strongly suggested that I abstain from watching movies or explicit television shows and from listening to "secular music." I suspect that the reason for such prohibitions was because my mentors in church knew that the innermost longings were hard to tame. If we split our longings between the world and the kingdom, it would eventually confuse us about what we truly longed for.

But such prohibitions narrow the Christian life to *what*. If you do this or do not do that, you will do Christianity well. I am not sure that is defensible with any careful reading of the Bible. Christianity is about a properly formed heart (or innermost being) that is marked by the character of Christ. What we yearn for—or as Jesus put it, what we seek—should be the kingdom first. The consumerism, hedonism, patriotism, and individualism that the world shapes us to long for are distractions from the kingdom of God.

The problem with the church's old ways of forming the *whats* of behavior is twofold: First, we do not live in a vacuum. For all the movies I missed, I still learned the secular longings of my friends every day in the hallway at school. Ignoring the culture did not accomplish what it was intended to do; after all, I went to public school, lived in a public neighborhood, played sports with "secular kids," and so on. Second, there is redemption in culture. If we look, we can find the narratives of the Christian faith in culture—even in surprising places. My favorite example is the AMC show *Breaking Bad*. The show begins with a modest high school chemistry teacher, Walter White, who learns he has cancer, fears for his family's long-term financial stability, and learns how easy it is for someone with his skill set to make methamphetamine. He decides to cook some drugs in order to store up cash for his family after his death. To his surprise, he goes into remission and now must deal with the consequences of his actions. He decides to double down on the villain he has cultivated, and he, as creator Vince Gilligan pitches, turns "Mr. Chips into Scarface."[1]

---

1. Genetta M. Adams, "'Breaking Bad': From Mr. Chips to Scarface in Ten Easy Steps," CNN.com, updated July 12, 2012, https://www.cnn.com/2012/07/12/showbiz/tv/breaking-bad-chips-scarface/index.html.

No one who watched *Breaking Bad* wanted to be like Walter White. He was a tragic character on an arc similar to a Shakespearean tragedy from the moment we meet him. Instead, a Christian watching with careful eyes could discern that this is the warning of sin's all-consuming nature. A simple poor choice with a good intention—making a batch of potent drugs so that his wife and children would be provided for when cancer took his life—led to him accidentally becoming a monster capable of murder.

This television show has a deeply developed theology of sin. In the show, we do not learn what not to do: we know not to cook drugs and sell them. Even drug dealers tend to know that it is wrong. We learn why: lives are destroyed, families are destroyed, fear sets in, innocent lives are decimated, and violence comes to reign in what were safe spaces. When we learn to care about the characters, we hurt when their lives are decimated by the sin of another.

Culture, I am afraid, is doing a better job speaking to the habitus of people than the church is. The church is still operating on the basis of information and obedience (not that either of those are inherently bad or wrong), while society is shaping people's innermost desires. Cultural liturgies are shaping people to be certain kinds of people and citizens. Regardless of whether we think culture is shaping people well or poorly, we must admit that liturgies are powerful for shaping how we react to life at a subconscious level.

Perhaps we are thinking, "What liturgies? Liturgies are what a certain kind of church (Catholic, Lutheran, Anglican, etc.) does." I would argue that all of life is liturgical, and Madison Avenue, Hollywood, and Washington DC are using better practices these days to shape us than the church currently is.

In worship, the church has historically used hymns, hymnals, creeds, confessionals, sermons, pilgrimages, and even incense as formational practices within the liturgy. Think of how the culture uses the same practices:

- **Hymns:** "The Star-Spangled Banner" (everyone must rise when sung!), "God Save the Queen" (English soccer players are lambasted in the media when they don't sing the song correctly—loud, demonstrative, proud!—before a big international match), "Macarena" (you have to do the dance!), "Watch Me!" (can you Whip and Nae Nae?)
- **Hymnals**: *Billboard* Top 40 lists, *Now That's What I Call Music! 73*, Casey Kasem/Ryan Seacrest Countdowns, "Best of" albums and lists
- **Creeds**: College fight songs, the Pledge of Allegiance, Boy or Girl Scout Promise
- **Confessionals**: Facebook, Twitter, Yik Yak, Anonymous articles to publications
- **Sermons**: podcasts, *TED Talks*, comedian tours, twenty-four-hour news channels
- **Pilgrimages**: Disney World, Wizarding World of Harry Potter, trips to stadiums of favorite teams, European vacation, Vegas weekends, Black Friday
- **Incense**: aromatherapy, Yankee Candles, Bath and Body Works
- **"Common Tables" or "Shared Life" (as an image for Communion or Eucharist)**: social media, Snapchat, Musical.ly, artisan food restaurants, YouTube, community gardens

This is not to say any of these are immoral. Most are morally neutral. However, our longing to participate in these practices is formational, and the invitations to practice these activities disciple our behavior and imagination. While we may not be worshipping, they are certainly liturgical acts that expect particular behaviors and outcomes.

Malcolm Gladwell posited what is known as the ten-thousand-hour rule. He points to the Beatles' famed gigs in Hamburg, Bill Gates's access to computers at the University of Washington in his younger years, and the unusual percentage of January birthdays among National Hockey League players, who as children, being older and bigger earlier than their peers, had more chances to play on youth all-star teams. These early practitioners of their crafts achieved mastery because they were able to reach ten thousand hours of practice. That is, for Gladwell, the level of expertise. He asserts that once an individual has practiced something for ten thousand hours, he or she is an expert.[2]

If there is any truth to Gladwell's theory, we are unlikely to achieve expertise in worship in our lifetime. If a Christian lives for eighty years and attends 1.5 hours of worship every Sunday of his or her life, that Christian will be in gathered worship for 6,240 hours.[3] Compare that to hours spent attending school, listening to the radio, watching the news, or catching movies. These other activities are likely dominating our formation.

If we are practicing heaven, practicing the kingdom when we gather to worship, we should perhaps be attentive to what Christian disciplines we are forming. We must be intentionally planning to help our people understand and experience at an innermost level the Christian life that God is calling us toward. The pastor, worship leader, musicians, and worship committee should take seriously not only what they plan but also why they plan it.

The church has a rich history of practices that speak not only to the rational mind but also to the body and the innermost being.

---

2. Malcolm Gladwell, *Outliers: The Story of Success* (New York: Little, Brown, 2008), 35-68.

3. 80x52x1.5=6,240.

There is a history of formation in Christian worship that we need to recall and tap into. This will require a new imagination and a recollection of the *why* of our practices. Let's journey together through the worship practices we know, and let's recall why we do what we do.

3
Call to Worship

• • •

How many times have you arrived at church—perhaps a little late—but the service has not begun. A worship leader stumbles on the stage, hurried, takes a deep breath, and says into the microphone, "Well, it's nice to have you here today."

Researchers say that the average Internet surfer decides within ten seconds if he or she will remain on a web page. Ten seconds! Does that mean in a world with ever-shortening attention spans that a person with a microphone has a similar span to hook the audience?

If this is the case, it would be prudent to take seriously the idea of a call to worship. Imagine a pastor, worship leader, or vocalist intentionally planning an engaging, passionate call to the gathered people of God that declares why they have gathered. Perhaps this is done by finding a psalm such as Psalm 100:

Shout for joy to the Lord, all the earth.
> Worship the Lord with gladness;
> come before him with joyful songs.

Know that the LORD is God.
>	It is he who made us, and we are his;
>	we are his people, the sheep of his pasture.
> Enter his gates with thanksgiving
>	and his courts with praise;
>	give thanks to him and praise his name.
> For the LORD is good and his love endures forever;
>	his faithfulness continues through all generations.

A text like this spurs hearers to remember why they have come. It draws attention from the world that is filled with bitterness, controversy, and partisanship to a space of joy and gladness. We are reminded that something different happens here, in the sanctuary of worship. We are called out of the world and into the worship of God.

This simple act of an intentional call to worship differs from many worship services I have attended. All too often, worship services begin haphazardly—late, sloppy, without direction. Instead, there should be a plan that is cohesive with the thematic thrust of the planned service. If it is Easter, turn the minds of the congregants toward the hope of the resurrection. If the theme is God's comfort in times of pain, share a stirring word of well-being with the people. If the theme of the day is the struggle for holiness, offer a word of lament or repentance to the people. Call the people from the humdrum of daily life to worship by directing them to the theme of the sermon.

Alexander Schmemann, an influential Orthodox priest, wrote a delightful book on the liturgical life of the people of God titled *For the Life of the World*. For Schmemann, all of the life of the church is liturgy pointed toward worship. We gather for liturgy as a coming together in one place bringing our lives with us. Gathering for worship is a leaving of our homes, beds, and lives in this present and concrete world. When we get in the car or walk down the road, we constitute the church of Christ. We enter into a new community with a new life. Time, life, and priorities are rearranged from this temporal world into that of the kingdom of Christ.[1]

So the leaving of life and coming to worship is the beginning of our sacramental time. We are leaving behind the narratives, liturgies, and toils of this world to attend to the heavenly, the kingdom. Schmemann reminds us what the early Christians realized, that to become the temple of the Holy Spirit, they must ascend to heaven where Christ has ascended.[2]

For Schmemann, the entrance into worship is not simply a coming into a bland sanctuary but a calling of the people to enter into the heavenly realm. This moment is the opportunity for the celebrant or pastor to call the people out of the world they know into a foretaste of the world that is to come. The call to worship is thus a means by which the pastor can point the community toward the kingdom of God. As pastors, let us not do this lightly, blandly, or routinely. Let us find words, enunciations, and proclamations that are worthy of the glorious kingdom of God! Let us call people from their lives, schedules, happenings, and dispositions to something celebration worthy, something otherworldly. Let us begin with a call to worship that calls them from this world into another.

And to those of us who are not the pastor or worship leader, let us come expecting that heaven is going to fall in this place. There is an epidemic of tardiness in the church today. If we are laypersons, let us show up early! Let us be prepared. Let us pray

---

1. Alexander Schmemann, *For the Life of the World: Sacraments and Orthodoxy* (Crestwood, NY: St. Vladimir's Seminary Press, 2002), 27.
2. Ibid., 28.

over pews and be in our seats when the service starts. We must model what we imagine heaven to be like in our preparation for Sunday morning.

In the church today, there is a growing guest mentality even among the membership. We are formed in our trips to Target, Chili's, and Amazon.com to believe that we are always right and that those places exist to serve us. This cultural liturgy has boiled over into the church. People leave churches because they are "not getting fed," as if the church exists solely to feed them. If we are not getting fed, we should probably get a better devotional book. Rather than looking for what the church can do for us, we should be intentional in reading the Scriptures, and we should come to church to serve, not to be served, as Jesus himself modeled for us. Some of us can take over the hospitality ministry; others can walk the aisles of the sanctuary and pray for all who will sit in the seats; and some can greet mothers in the parking lot and offer to carry a bag. We all can help others experience the transition from the secular to the holy.

When the minister walks to the pulpit and invites the congregation to worship, by all means, we should be present and expecting. The call to worship is a call to transition from the secular. It is a call to turn from the world toward the holy. It is anticipatory. We are called from our routine lives to the important work of worship. Our attention should be given to God, and our lives brought to this work. We are called to lift our hearts and lives to God, expecting that God's presence will descend upon us.

God is faithful to come to a gathered group of the worshipping church. This worship time is a glorious happening—that of heaven meeting earth. The call to worship is a vital invitation that we should take seriously, both as minister and congregation. But to do so, the minister must engage in intentional planning and enthusiasm, and the congregation must arrive with the intention to be present and engaged. Let's not miss this meaningful invitation to turn our faces from the world toward heaven because we have come to this moment with a haphazard expectation of God's call.

4
Singing

• • •

Have you ever been to Beverly Hills? My wife, Charryse, and I went to Beverly Hills years ago. When we go on vacation, we rent a car—the cheapest car possible. And so we drove a motorized cardboard box on wheels when we visited California. I remember driving through Beverly Hills, and two things really made an impression on me: The first was this expensive car, driven by a young driver, that approached us from behind. It was going about eighty miles an hour in a twenty-five-mile-an-hour zone, and it weaved around us as if the young driver didn't have a care in the world; it was terrifying. The second was the feeling that I was dodging police officers who wanted to banish me from a place I did not belong.

Beverly Hills is an exclusive culture in America. We know the zip code: 90210. We know about Beverly Hills, because it is where entertainment stars live and where television programs are set. It is a place beyond our grasp—a place that, if we go, we won't even feel we belong.

Weezer wrote and performed a song titled "Beverly Hills"; the lyrics grappled with this exclusive culture of rich America. The song is about a guy who wants more out of life. He understands himself to be lower-class and not quite good enough. Looking at the Instagrammable and wealthy public, he thinks he would like to be someone others would want to photograph by a pool. He wants a fit body, a well-to-do life, and a huge house; in short, he wants to be one of the "pretty" people. He wants to be part of something bigger than his reality.

After dreaming about extreme cleanliness, hired hands, celebrities, and beautiful people, the singer comes to grip with his circumstances. He realizes he has no chance to live the life of wealth and fame he desires. So he decides to be happy the way he is, observing celebrities from afar.[1]

This is what we do in society, right? We love our reality television shows. We love it when famous people subject themselves to cameras and demonstrate how they just play through life. We have, in many ways, in our own culture, lost our ability to play because we would rather sit in front of the TV and watch other people play. This pastime of watching others appeals to a wide range of age groups, from adults reading the *National Enquirer* to children viewing other children on YouTube playing Legos and video games. This song probes our angst as people, how we want to be part of something bigger than our everyday lives. And yet we often aim for places we still don't belong.

Now, what's interesting about coming to church is that it's not like Beverly Hills. It's not an exclusive culture, nor is it meant to be. It's a place where we come to be a part of something bigger

---

1. Weezer, "Beverly Hill," by Rivers Cuomo, recorded 2004, track 1 on *Make Believe*, Geffen Records B0004520-01, 2005, vinyl LP.

than ourselves, but we find that we *do* belong, that all are welcome, that everyone has a voice. And that voice is so often easily found in our singing. In our singing, everyone's voice matters. As we gather together, and as the music plays and we sing, we find that we are corporately lifted to a higher place. That lifting is God pulling us toward himself, and God's kingdom becomes alive as we worship. We find that God's kingdom is not like Beverly Hills. Instead, God's kingdom draws near and invites people who are lowly, saying to them, "You have an important place in this kingdom, and you are invited to experience it when the congregation sings."

Music is interesting, because while we may not "get" the music, it still stirs something within us, positive or negative. Even with music in a foreign language or an unfamiliar style, we know music when we hear it! It is ubiquitous because every culture uses music in some way to identify itself. Music is also profoundly important because it evokes a response from deep within us: How many times have you encountered a song whose message or theme spoke for you? We also use music to embed, deep within us, memories, beliefs, and emotions.

Think of how music works in advertising. The jingles in commercials are meant to seep down within us so that the sounds and lyrics become perpetual messages inside us.

"Break me off a piece of that Kit Kat bar."

"I don't wanna grow up."

"My bologna has a first name, it's O-S-C-A-R."

Thirty seconds of airtime produces a lifetime of advertising within the recesses of our minds. Our subconscious reminds us of our cravings for Kit Kat bars, Toys "R" Us, and Oscar Mayer bologna.

Songs become extremely important means of communication and information sharing. We use songs to remember things. My daughters had the same second grade teacher, two years apart from one another. Their classroom teacher would take songs from the radio that all the kids knew and rework concepts that they were studying in class into those songs. She would take a Taylor Swift or Katy Perry song and rewrite the lyrics to help them understand sharing or fractions. The teacher was using music to help children recall information and to come up with new ideas. Music has that power to help us with such things. This is one of the reasons we sing in church! Because so much of what we believe about God we learned by singing in our youth. The songs we choose for worship, we hope, are grounded in biblical reality and truth. When we sing those songs, they help us remember who God is and what God is doing. Our Christian walk and our Christian faith become so intertwined with what we sing.

A church I pastored would hold several remote nursing-home services. Occasionally, I would be asked to go and preach and sing with our elderly friends. Every time I went, I tried to sing great hymns of the church: "Amazing Grace," "How Great Thou Art," "Blessed Assurance," and so on. Every time those folks gathered for church, they would listen as I sang a terrible solo for them and then ask if they could please sing "Jesus Loves Me." I would agree, and the room would burst with song. For those homebound elderly, this was not a child's song; it was a memory—a memory of who Jesus was to them when they were little and who Jesus remained to them today. The words may have been embedded in their minds and hearts decades ago, but the truth felt fresh to them. Our songs become our theologies.[2] This has been true throughout our faith's

---

2. It seems important to note that this should not become an argument for hymn-only singing. While I personally adore many of the hymns I grew up singing, I equally love some of the songs that have been written and introduced into Christian hymnody in my adult years. Time should not be the judge of our music. Songs

history. The Psalms are ancient songs of the Jews. Pliny, the second-century Roman governor of what is now Turkey, wanted to identify the Christians in his territory, but all he could discern was that they were a group of people who gathered before sunrise to sing to Christ "as to a god."[3]

Jesus sang as well. The Psalms were known by all of the Jews. As Jesus was dying on the cross, he said, "My God, my God, why have you forsaken me?" (Matt. 27:46). Taken at face value, these words are difficult for us to understand. The Greek word translated "forsaken" means "abandoned" or "left alone," and it's almost as if Jesus is crying, "Where are you God? Where have you been? Why aren't you helping me now?" For us, as readers, we are tempted to say, "Well, if God's going to help anyone, wouldn't Jesus be the one most likely to be helped? What is happening?" Jesus's questioning the whereabouts of God unsettles us. Context does not set everything right, but it does guide us.

Most of us who were raised in church or who have attended a Christian funeral know Psalm 23: "The Lord is my shepherd; I shall not want" (v. 1, KJV). One need not cite Psalm 23 in most Christian circles. Simply saying the words "The Lord is my shepherd" would send most of us to the correct page of the Bible. The psalm before the famous Psalm 23, Psalm 22, begins with similarly compelling words: "My God, my God, why have you forsaken me?" (v. 1).

Just as we call to mind the entirety of Psalm 23 when we hear the first verse, Jesus is recalling Psalm 22 by reciting its beginning. While Jesus is on the cross, he's hearing the words of his youth from this song again, embedded within his memory, and these

---

should be discerned through our theological lenses. Are these songs pointing our people in the direction that we yearn for them to be in Christ?

3. Pliny the Younger, "Pliny to the Emperor Trajan," GeorgeTown.edu, accessed March 27, 2020, http://faculty.georgetown.edu/jod/texts/pliny.html.

words comfort him. Even though he feels forsaken by God, he understands God's salvation can work through his forsakenness. Listen to the words of Psalm 22:

> My God, my God, why have you forsaken me?
>> Why are you so far from saving me,
>> so far from my cries of anguish?
>
> My God, I cry out by day, but you do not answer,
>> by night, but I find no rest.
>
> Yet you are enthroned as the Holy One;
>> you are the one Israel praises.
>
> In you our ancestors put their trust;
>> they trusted and you delivered them.
>
> To you they cried out and were saved;
>> in you they trusted and were not put to shame.
>
> But I am a worm and not a man,
>> scorned by everyone, despised by the people.
>
> All who see me mock me;
>> they hurl insults, shaking their heads.
>
> "He trusts in the LORD," they say,
>> "let the LORD rescue him.
>
> Let him deliver him,
>> since he delights in him."
>
> Yet you brought me out of the womb;
>> you made me trust in you, even at my mother's breast.
>
> From birth I was cast on you;
>> from my mother's womb you have been my God.
>
> Do not be far from me,
>> for trouble is near
>> and there is no one to help.

Many bulls surround me;
> strong bulls of Bashan encircle me.
Roaring lions that tear their prey
> open their mouths wide against me.
I am poured out like water,
> and all my bones are out of joint.
My heart has turned to wax;
> it has melted within me.
My mouth is dried up like a potsherd,
> and my tongue sticks to the roof of my mouth;
> you lay me in the dust of death.

Dogs surround me,
> a pack of villains encircles me;
> they pierce my hands and my feet.
All my bones are on display;
> people stare and gloat over me.
They divide my clothes among them
> and cast lots for my garment.

But you, LORD, do not be far from me.
> You are my strength; come quickly to help me.
Deliver me from the sword,
> my precious life from the power of the dogs.
Rescue me from the mouth of the lions;
> save me from the horns of the wild oxen.

I will declare your name to my people;
> in the assembly I will praise you.
You who fear the LORD, praise him!
>> All you descendants of Jacob, honor him!
>> Revere him, all you descendants of Israel!
For he has not despised or scorned

> the suffering of the afflicted one;
> he has not hidden his face from him
> > but has listened to his cry for help.
>
> From you comes the theme of my praise in the great assembly;
> > before those who fear you I will fulfill my vows.
> The poor will eat and be satisfied;
> > those who seek the LORD will praise him—
> > may your hearts live forever!
>
> All the ends of the earth
> > will remember and turn to the LORD,
> and all the families of the nations
> > will bow down before him,
> for dominion belongs to the LORD
> > and he rules over the nations.
>
> All the rich of the earth will feast and worship;
> > all who go down to the dust will kneel before him—
> > those who cannot keep themselves alive.
> Posterity will serve him;
> > future generations will be told about the Lord.
> They will proclaim his righteousness,
> > declaring to a people yet unborn:
> > He has done it! (Vv. 1-31)

Did you catch the multiple images in that psalm—written hundreds of years before Jesus's crucifixion—that match Jesus's experiences on the cross? Images such as bones out of joint, pierced hands and feet, and intense thirst fit the psalm and Jesus's crucifixion and suffering.

It's right for Christ to say, "My God, why have you abandoned me here? Why have you left me for this?" It's right for him to feel abandoned, but when he feels abandoned, when he feels forsaken, he remembers a song he memorized as a child at temple. That song-psalm finally declares that through the suffering of the Righteous One future generations will learn about God. It affirms that the one who suffers is not far from God. God has not turned his back on the sufferer. When we are suffering, our suffering does not distance us from God, but God works toward salvation through and from the suffering. And it's a song on the lips of Jesus on the cross that recognizes the possibility of the salvation of all people, that while he feels abandoned as he suffers, God's work is not yet finished. The song comforts him, and it pushes him through; it's a song that helps Jesus remember who he is, whose he is, and why he does what he does. He remembers and declares that God saves the suffering. It's a song that accomplishes this juxtaposition of pain and hope for Jesus in his passion.

We continue to sing in church because the songs become ways of remembering, when remembering is hard. Whether it's because our memories are aging or because suffering blurs our vision of ourselves, the songs we sing together in worship help us recall who and whose we are when we are no longer surrounded by the body of Christ. Those songs also provide us hope for what is to come. They remind us that where we are now is not the final destination of the Christian life. We sing about a kingdom that is here now but is yet to come in its fullness—a kingdom coming to us through the death and resurrection of Christ. We sing that though there is struggle and pain now, we will spend eternity with God. We sing not only about our present situation but also about a world in which we have not yet fully participated.

And that kingdom that is here but not yet in its fullness is singing even now, though beyond our comprehension. Our singing joins that of the saints, angels, and patriarchs. In the book of Revelation, John peers into the heavenly throne room and sees them singing songs of praise. In chapter 14, when the 144,000 are gathered, they sing a new song, accompanied by harpists.

When we sing at church, we join with the heavens in singing. In fact, we are practicing the kingdom as we sing. Don Saliers, a professor of worship at Candler School of Theology, describes worship as the descending of the glory of God into the space of praise the people of God lift up. Our singing in worship does not exist divorced from the praise being offered in heaven.[4]

The classic movie *Back to the Future* helps us to see how this can be. Marty McFly travels into the past, concerned that his parents will not get together. If they don't get together, he and his siblings will cease to exist, thus altering the future. There is a critical moment when Marty's parents are at a dance and in danger of missing the kiss that caused them to fall in love and get married. Marty's job is to make sure they kiss.

Marty arrives (his parents unaware that he is their future son) and plays the guitar at the school dance in question. As he plays the song "Earth Angel," he slowly begins losing his existence; his body is weakening and disappearing because his parents do not seem to be getting together. At just the right moment, his dad punches the bad guy impeding the couple and kisses Marty's future mother. Marty's existence—his life—is fully restored.

Ecstatic at what has happened, Marty bursts out in a song of joy. Does this sound familiar? Isn't this what we do in church when we discover we have a life in Christ that we didn't expect? Just like Marty, we want to sing a song of joy! So Marty sings "Johnny B. Goode" by Chuck Berry. But it's a song from another world; the song doesn't exist yet in the world of the past that he is visiting.

---

4. Don E. Saliers, *Worship as Theology: Foretaste of Glory Divine* (Nashville: Abingdon Press, 1994).

So Marty directs the band with a couple of chords and tells them to follow him. Marty proceeds to play this "otherworldly" song. Everyone begins dancing. The audience likes it—at first, but the more Marty gets into it, the more he behaves like someone from a world yet to come, and the more the audience is put off by it.

There may come a point in our lives when we're still singing and the rest of the world has stopped. Others may look at us as if we're strange. We may wonder if we have become strange. But Christians who have tasted the kingdom not of this world keep singing—even when it is awkward and lonely.

The church sings so that the joy of the Lord will pour out. People who do not know the fullness of the Christian life or the kingdom of God may love the beginning of the song—but they may not be ready for the rest of it. We must keep the church singing. The songs we sing are about a world that hasn't fully revealed itself yet, but it is coming. Singing with joy helps us discover that we are becoming who we are in Christ while we sing! The words and melodies of the songs become the realities of our lives. Our truths are narrated there, and they accompany us as we leave the sanctuary. When struggle or suffering comes, those otherworldly songs may surprise us with comfort or hope. This practice of singing shapes and forms us into the people God is calling us to be.

5
Reading Scripture
• • •

Does it strike you as strange that Scripture is read aloud in church when almost everyone in the room owns a Bible—and could simply read it on his or her own? Reading Scripture aloud is an ancient practice. The scrolls of the Old Testament were read in synagogues, the Gospels were passed from church to church and read before each congregation, Paul's letters were read to the whole church, and the book of Revelation was recited and performed in church gatherings. Some of this was for practical reasons—not everyone was literate.

One may wonder if, in the twenty-first century, we are on the precipice of a new illiteracy. Though people still read, the availability of video has made extensive reading rare for many; the shorter written interactions on social media often draw more readers than do books and other longer writings. For example, Twitter dispenses capsules in 280 characters or less. Problems can arise when information sources are too narrow. Facebook, for instance, has a button that allows unsourced, biased material to be shared with a simple click. The ease of transferring information today allows for fast decisions based on bias as much as fact. Our insistence on receiving information quickly, as well as our disinterest in reading lengthy compositions, creates an intellectualism of sound bites that hinders us from engaging in critical thinking.

Reading Scripture in church invites people from a society that is reading less, in shorter form, to sit for a time and listen to a text and allow it to saturate their thoughts and presence.

But we also are reminded in corporate gatherings that the text is about more than any personal application or interpretation: when we read it together, we are called to something that has been read to the people of God for several millennia. The responsibility of applying the text extends beyond just relating it to individuals in the here and now. This is a living, breathing document that has enlivened, admonished, and nourished the church long before we came to it.

This quickly becomes a source of tension for those who are wooed and wowed by the new. We line up outside of Apple stores, armed with $1,000 for portable phones marginally better than the ones we already have. We shop racks filled with 60 percent discounts because the design is "last season." We yearn to feel fresh, young, and novel. In fact, we idolize youth.

The idolization of youth is why movie stars date people half their age. Despite age discrimination laws, people sometimes lose their jobs because of their age. Television networks make shows that score well with the eighteen-to-thirty-five demographic, while ignoring other age groups. As a result, when we get to the point that we no longer feel young, we can look back to our youth and exclaim, "Those were the good ole days!"

During my sophomore year in college, I was walking through the mall in the city where I had attended high school, and I saw a girl from my high school class, a former cheerleader. We were both twenty, and she confessed, "I miss high school; those were the best days of our lives." She was serious too! Bruce Springsteen shares similar sentiments in his song "Glory Days." The lyrics say that the days gone by are just boring stories to tell. There's nothing to do, now that you've had kids, but to put them to bed, work till you can work no more, and imagine how the days used to be better.[1]

It's a depressing song put to exciting music, so we listen to it and think we are having fun. Yet the story is about people who are no longer satisfied with their lives. They used to feel gratified when they were young and had a strong arm and/or were attractive. Now they have nothing but boring stories of "glory days." Think about how often we run into this subversive narrative: When we were young was when we mattered! Youth or the past was the best part of our lives.

Maybe that's become the narrative in the church. We talk about the "glory days" of the past, when the church was younger. We remember when God *used* to speak, we remember when God *used* to rule, and we remember when we *used* to worship "that way." Those were the glory days! But now we don't really *feel* it anymore: "it" is no longer the way "it" was. We would rather go back to the glory days of our relationship with God than to hear God speak fresh and new today. This is how the culture's false narrative of youth creeps into our church and grabs hold of the way we understand worship.

Why, then, do we read Scripture aloud in our worship gatherings? After all, it is ironic that the Scriptures we read are ancient stories of how God acted in the past. Those stories are two thou-

---

1. Bruce Springsteen, "Glory Days," recorded May 5, 1982, track 4 of side 2 on *Born in the U.S.A.*, Columbia QC 38653, 1984, vinyl LP.

sand-plus years old, and we read them as if they matter while we are seeking a fresh revelation of God.

Elevating reading to an important place in the church, in itself, is a countercultural practice. In high school and middle school, reading stories and books was vitally important to our formation and understanding. One of the earliest ways that I came to learn about the dangers of racism was from reading the book *To Kill a Mockingbird* by Harper Lee. It is the story of Tom Robinson, an African American, who is falsely accused of raping a white girl after she tries to seduce him. The whole town rallies around the girl's story, but the reader sees the world through the eyes of Scout, the daughter of Tom's defense attorney, Atticus Finch. The reader is invited to realize how terrible racism is. Many American adolescent students learned to combat racism by reading *To Kill a Mockingbird*.

Many young people also learned in school the evils of the inequities of Communism by reading the satirical novel *Animal Farm*. That book was actually written by a socialist, George Orwell, who looked into the Soviet Union and saw it to be a dangerous society; he wrote the famous line "All animals are equal, but some animals are more equal than others."[2] That was his critique of Communism. A whole generation of young Americans and Britons, terrified by the Cold War, came to understand Communism as evil and an enemy through the reading of this story.

Many Americans learned to combat the labeling of others by reading the book *The Scarlet Letter*. This story by Nathaniel Hawthorne is about a society that branded a young woman who had sinned. Readers learned about the dangers of labeling people without knowing the full story.

---

2. George Orwell, *Animal Farm* (London: Secker and Warburg, 1945), chap. 10.

Many of us had to read the writings of Charles Dickens. His stories *Great Expectations*, *A Christmas Carol*, and so on, are almost always about the class struggle between the rich and poor. Young Britons read those stories and thus gain a better understanding of their society.

Reading stories helps us formulate the way we see the world. Reading helps us understand the world we live in and how to react to it. And so it is for us, the people of God. We gather together to read the Scriptures, that they may be foundational stories for us. The stories that have been handed down about God's interactions with humans are not merely stories about the past but also formational tools; they help us understand what the people of God do that pleases God and what they do that displeases God.

Reading these stories is not to acquire a history lesson, nor is it an opportunity to look back at the glory days and say, "It was really good when God acted back then!" Instead, reading gives us a chance to gather together to hear the Word of the Lord and say, with a fresh revelation, that God, "who is, and who was, and who is to come" (Rev. 1:8), is the same God now as then. The way that God acted and behaved in the stories points to how God acts and wants to be among us today. God is shaping us in the reading of these stories. As we look back and read the Gospel texts, we are given prime seats for viewing how Jesus was in this world. We should not come away from the text saying that Jesus was a good guy or even that he was a good God. We say that Jesus is God, who came to live among us, and that through the resurrection still lives among us and continues to act. We read the stories of the Old Testament, and we see God calling people from sin to repentance and restoration. We see how communities marked as followers of God are called to live likewise. We are invited to mourn our own sin, think critically about how to live as the people of God, and seek repentance and restoration with God. These stories are given to us so we can see God's activity in our lives and in our community.

There is a biblical story about reading Scripture aloud that leads to the response of repentance and restoration. It is a story that happened during the reign of the Persian king Artaxerxes, while the Israelites were in exile. As you may recall, God had become weary of the sin of his people, so he allowed the Babylonians to sack Jerusalem and remove people from the promised land, forcing them to live in Babylon. Later the Persians supplanted the Babylonians and ruled over the exiled Israelites. Some of the well-known stories from the exile include the account of Daniel in the lions' den and the rescue of Shadrach, Meshach, and Abednego from the fiery furnace. Such stories illustrate what the Israelites faced while in a foreign land where foreign gods were worshipped. During the exile, the Israelites not only came to grips with their sin but also considered what they ought to do in an alien land. Were they to make things right with their God and seek forgiveness from him and restoration? Or were they to consider themselves part of the new culture and people among whom they lived? Should they worship the foreign gods? Feeling lost in exile, the Israelites, on the one hand, yearned for the past when they lived in the promised land, where God was God and they were free to worship him. But on the other hand, they felt they had to get along in the foreign land where they now were.

In the church today, a conversation has emerged connecting the exile of Israel to the current situation of the church.[3] Back in the "glory days" of the church, God was perceived near because people prayed in schools and talked about God and the Christian

---

3. See T. Scott Daniels, *Embracing Exile: Living Faithfully as God's Unique People in the World* (Kansas City: Beacon Hill Press of Kansas City, 2017).

faith in everyday society. Now it seems as if we live in a foreign land where things are different. The question is, How does God work in exile? If we are in exile today, how do we see God at work, and is God asking us to look back to the glory days and say, "Oh, I wish it was like that again"? Or is God cultivating a fresh vision to invite us out of exile? The story in question, set during the reign of King Artaxerxes, addresses these very issues. It is about raising up a fresh vision from exile that leads to repentance and restoration.

Nehemiah, the Israelite cupbearer to King Artaxerxes, one day asks some travelers about the state of things back in Jerusalem. The travelers report that the walls are in rubble, the gates were burned, and the people are greatly troubled. Nehemiah's heart becomes incredibly heavy, and he hurts.

One day the king sees Nehemiah looking downcast and asks, "What is happening?" Nehemiah tells him about his homeland in rubble and that he does not know what to do. King Artaxerxes allows Nehemiah to return to Jerusalem with the authority of governor to rebuild the city walls and restore the gates (ca. 446 BC).

Upon arriving in Jerusalem, Nehemiah sets to work rebuilding the city's walls and gates. Despite threats and interference from surrounding communities, Nehemiah succeeds with the rebuilding plans. Earlier, two groups of Israelites had returned from exile. The first group worked on rebuilding the temple, which was completed under the reign of Darius (515 BC); the next returnees, led by Ezra (sent by Artaxerxes), sought to restore the law of Moses and enact reforms (ca. 458 BC). So now both the temple and the city walls are restored, many people have returned to the promised land, and Ezra's reforms are underway.

In the light of these events, Ezra reads the law of Moses before the people. Many generations have passed since Moses received the law given him from God for these people, God's people. Now the people struggle as they gather to hear the law because their failure to follow the law is directly related to their going into exile. The reading of the law will be corrective and hard to hear. Yet they gather around and invite Ezra, the keeper of the law, to read it to them anew. The story of what unfolds is found in Nehemiah 8:

> All the people came together as one in the square before the Water Gate. They told Ezra the teacher of the Law to bring out the Book of the Law of Moses, which the LORD had commanded for Israel.
>
> So on the first day of the seventh month Ezra the priest brought the Law before the assembly, which was made up of men and women and all who were able to understand. He read it aloud from daybreak till noon as he faced the square before the Water Gate in the presence of the men, women and others who could understand. And all the people listened attentively to the Book of the Law.
>
> Ezra the teacher of the Law stood on a high wooden platform built for the occasion. Beside him on his right stood Mattithiah, Shema, Anaiah, Uriah, Hilkiah and Maaseiah; and on his left were Pedaiah, Mishael, Malkijah, Hashum, Hashbaddanah, Zechariah and Meshullam.
>
> Ezra opened the book. All the people could see him because he was standing above them; and as he opened it, the people all stood up. Ezra praised the LORD, the great God; and all the people lifted their hands and responded, "Amen! Amen!" Then they bowed down and worshiped the LORD with their faces to the ground.
>
> The Levites—Jeshua, Bani, Sherebiah, Jamin, Akkub, Shabbethai, Hodiah, Maaseiah, Kelita, Azariah, Jozabad, Hanan and Pelaiah—instructed the people in the Law while the people were standing there. They read from the Book of

the Law of God, making it clear and giving the meaning so that the people understood what was being read.

Then Nehemiah the governor, Ezra the priest and teacher of the Law, and the Levites who were instructing the people said to them all, "This day is holy to the LORD your God. Do not mourn or weep." For all the people had been weeping as they listened to the words of the Law.

Nehemiah said, "Go and enjoy choice food and sweet drinks, and send some to those who have nothing prepared. This day is holy to our Lord. Do not grieve, for the joy of the LORD is your strength."

The Levites calmed all the people, saying, "Be still, for this is a holy day. Do not grieve."

Then all the people went away to eat and drink, to send portions of food and to celebrate with great joy, because they now understood the words that had been made known to them. (Vv. 1-18)

Imagine their position. Before this reading, the people looked at what had happened to them and wondered where God was. And now God is being revealed in the reading of an ancient text. It reminds them of who they have been for generations and who they will be. And the only response they have to the public reading of Scripture is crying—just absolute, out-of-control crying, as they understand and rehear who God is calling them to be. They don't cry because they hear the law of Moses and just think that God was good back then. They don't consider the time of Moses and the exodus to be the "glory days." They understand in the reading of the Scripture that God is calling them to be his people moving forward. They must change; they must be different. So they begin to meet often to read the law, and when they read the law, they read it for a quarter of the day and then spend the next quarter repenting. They repent for the sins of their fathers, themselves, and the nation of Israel. They do so, not because God "was," but because of who the Scriptures tell them they are going to be.

One of the defining movies of Generation X was *The Breakfast Club*. *The Breakfast Club* is the story of several high school teens who are all very different: the rich little princess, the delinquent, the jock, the geek, and the introvert. These teens end up together in Saturday detention. Not any of them think they belong there. During the day, they learn that the "rich princess" doesn't have it as easy as it seems. They discover that the delinquent was given only a packet of smokes for Christmas by his dad. As they begin to share their stories, they begin to see why they create facades to hide behind. As the day unfolds, they begin to tear down their personal walls and show who they really are. No matter what society labels them, they find the humanity they share with each other. They begin to look at each other differently.

As the story ends, the teens all leave Saturday detention with the incredible boldness that they now truly know each other. But the question is, When Monday comes, can they treat one another as they did on Saturday? Can they live out the new truths they learned in detention?

This is the same challenge we have in church when we gather around the Scriptures. When Scripture is read, we are reminded of who God is and who God is calling us to be. Surprisingly, we find that we allow Scripture to read us as well. It invites us to repentance—literally, to turn around and become the people that God is calling us to be. The question is then placed upon us, Now that we know who God is, as he is revealed in the Scriptures, can we live that way on Monday?

Scripture is transformative and not just a collection of ancient literature. These words enliven and enrich us to be something new, created and re-created by God, as we leave the sanctuary.

It is hard to invite the text to read us as we are reading or listening to it. Scripture calls us to a countercultural life. But we're not left to this task on our own. The same Holy Spirit that inspired writers to write about what God was doing in their world, the timeless Spirit that helped give us the Scriptures, is working to inspire us to have eyes to see and ears to hear what the Lord is doing among the people of his church.

6
Prayer
• • •

One reason that the Beatles stagnated—along with relational struggles and their increased drug usage—was because John Lennon famously said that the Beatles had become more popular than Jesus. Their subsequent American tour was marked by sagging attendances, firecrackers going off on stage, and protests. The ill-advised comment contributed to the Beatles becoming a studio-only band.

John Lennon always maintained a fandom. But after the breakup, he entered a posthippie phase with his new wife, Yoko Ono, that seemed to be best defined in his song "Imagine." The lyrics ask the listener to envision or "imagine" what it would be like if heaven, hell, countries, and religion did not exist—that is, if there were no divisions and no conflict, just peace and unity.[1]

Some theological quibbling can be done here. John Lennon has no theology of sin, and his eschatology is questionable—that

---

1. John Lennon, vocalist, "Imagine," by John Lennon and Yoko Ono, recorded 1971, track 1 of side 1 on *Imagine*, Apple Records SW 3379, 1971, vinyl LP.

by our imaginations, imagining a better place, we can overcome just by the power within us.

As a pastor, I obviously believe religion is important, so we start on different planes. Yet despite some of the initial issues in this song, there is something helpful for us within the lyrics: this idea of imagining a place, a way of life, that is different from our own and then reacting to that imagined place by behaving in accordance with it.

This is compatible with what Jesus invited us to do in the Lord's Prayer and the Sermon on the Mount. Jesus, himself, paints an image of what the kingdom of God looks like. We, the people of God, are invited to live into that kingdom, on earth as it is in heaven.

Fortunately for us, Revelation 4–5 gives us a vantage point for viewing what is happening in heaven. The "twenty-four elders," "four living creatures," multitudes of angels, and "every creature" surround the throne and the triumphant slaughtered Lamb, giving proper glory to God.

Imagine, if we may borrow the idea from John Lennon, that what is in heaven is on earth as well. In the Lord's Prayer, Jesus specifically instructs his followers, who are asking how to pray, to pray that it would be on earth as it is in heaven. That is the yearning he seeks to instill in our lives: adoration and glory to God here and now, like that of Revelation 4–5.

Interestingly, Jesus instructs his followers to pray in private to avoid being showy (Matt. 6:5-8). Jesus is telling us that prayer is not a time for flashy display, nor is it a time to demonstrate how spiritual, well-spoken, or in touch with God we think we are. God knows what we need before we say it. The apostle Paul says that the Spirit groans with words that are indiscernible, interceding for us (Rom. 8:26-27). So why do we do pray publicly in worship? Does that go against Jesus's instructions?

No, unless it becomes a flashy display. Instead, this time should facilitate an indelible connection with the living God, made manifest among the gathered believers in worship. What we imagine heaven to look like, colored by Revelation 4–5, becomes the scene we find ourselves in. We are able, as a gathered people, to speak into the ear of our Lord, who has visited us.

In corporate prayer, we take a rare moment to pray beyond what comes to our minds. Certainly, our individual crises matter, and we pray for those, but we also become aware of what is weighing on others. We see folks weeping at an altar, we recall the cancer surgery our sister in Christ is facing, we learn about the financial pinch of the family who lost a job, or we remember the prodigal son or daughter that parents are hoping will return to the fold.

Corporate prayer also has several very important formational aspects, as we mirror the activities of heaven in our local gathering. First, we pray to the same slaughtered Lamb who is in heaven, revealed to us in the book of Revelation. This prayer is a reminder that the Lamb who has been slain is present among us. Second, as the pastor intercedes for the people, he or she models praying for those who wonder how to pray. Pastors who yearn to be showy in their prayers are in danger of violating Christ's warning and are forming prayers who become showy as well. Finally, corporate prayer moves us past our routine, potentially individualistic petitions. We see the needs among us, and we are reminded to pray for others as well as ourselves. As you can see, corporate prayer shapes us into Christian people who are present in the presence of Christ, humble in speaking to Christ, and communal in faith.

God knows our needs, our hurts, our pain, our medical concerns—all our needs before we mention them. Prayer is relational. If you had a friend who solely told you what they needed all the time, that friendship would not last long. Friendship is a give-and-take; it's a working together, a hearing and speaking. And so often, our prayer life is about us speaking and—I hate to say it—treating God a bit as if he's a genie. It's as if our Bible is our lamp, and if we rub it well enough, God will hear our prayers and respond.

That's not really what's going on here. In fact, the prayer Jesus tells us to pray is scandalous. It scandalizes us and our perspective—it really, really does! If it didn't, Jesus wouldn't need to redirect us to it! Right? But the prayer itself has almost become second nature to us; we have it memorized. Although it's almost commonplace for us, the words themselves are weighty and almost difficult, if we really think about it. We even start, after Jesus told us to pray quietly and in secret (Matt. 6:5-8), with the word "Our"—"Our Father." Well, he's already outdone us, because what we want to pray is, "My Father"! What we want to pray is "From my perspective, let it be done, God," but we begin by saying that we join together in prayer. "We, your people, all pray—in our own closet, in our own home, at our own dinner table, in our own church." Whether you are by yourself or in community, you are praying to a God who is shared by his people across the world and across time; he is shared by those who have died in the Lord and those who are yet to be born. This God to whom we're praying is not concerned about "my" perspective but about "our" perspective.

"Our Father which art in heaven, Hallowed be thy name!" (Matt. 6:9, KJV). "Holiness" is your name. You are "holy"; you are "hallowed"—those are big words. And so we say, "Hallowed be thy name. Thy kingdom come. Thy will be done in earth, as it is in heaven" (vv. 9-10, KJV). These words point back to our discussion about the throne room. And what I think John Lennon does well for us here is to remind us that we have an imagination. We can imagine beyond what is. And so, what Jesus is telling us to imagine is the throne room of heaven, where the Father is with his Son, who was crucified and raised to life, and the Holy Spirit. It's where the persons of the Trinity love and joyfully dance together. Jesus is saying, "Pray that this joy and love of God breaks into our world in a mighty way."

We don't have to live in the status quo. We don't have to look around and say, "Well, I can't wait 'til Jesus comes back and destroys this whole thing we've set up; it's a mess around here!" And so often, that's how we talk as Christian people: "This world is a mess; we need him to come back!" But Jesus is saying, "Imagine where God's throne is, and pray that the way it is there would come on earth!" That's a radical prayer, is it not? That is a daring prayer to pray, and yet it's the very prayer that Jesus suggests we pray. It's not about ending this world because it's a mess but about saying, "O Lord, could you make it here like it is where your throne is?" Do we have an imagination for what that could look like?

If not, read the Sermon on the Mount. When Jesus is giving the Sermon on the Mount, he's talking about kingdom ethics, the way life is lived in his kingdom. The way we will live in his heaven is how we should be living now! And so, he's not speaking allegorically about loving our enemies or about forgiving our neighbor because God will in like manner forgive us; he's speaking quite literally. He's not kidding when he tells us not to worry about tomorrow. He's not exaggerating when he admonishes us not to store up treasures on earth, where they can decay or be destroyed. He's not jesting about not committing adultery or about not seeking an eye for an eye. He's serious when he tells us to go the extra mile and to turn the other cheek.

If we have a hard time imagining what the kingdom looks like when we pray "your kingdom come, your will be done, on earth as it is in heaven" (Matt. 6:10), the Sermon on the Mount can restir our imagination. We should stop thinking that the way of life portrayed in the Sermon on the Mount is only for hyper-Christians but not realistic for all Christians. The idea is daunting, but the gift of Christlikeness is given by grace, a free gift of God to those who are open to it. Becoming Christlike—embodying the ethics of the coming kingdom revealed in Jesus's sermon—can be slow, but it is realistic for us all.

William Willimon, the Methodist pastor, scholar, and bishop, once wrote, "To be Christian is to learn to see the world in a certain way, until day by day, I become as I see."[2] Praying is a critical task in this work. When we pray, we are imagining who God is and, in relationship, asking God who we are in light of who he is. We are telling him our needs and our wants, but we are also seeking to hear what he has to say. More than anything, though, prayer is a tangible recognition that the living Christ is present in our midst, and we have his ear. In worship, prayer reminds us that the imaginative life—rooted in the vision cast by the Sermon on the Mount—is lived empowered by a God who dwells near us, hears us, and speaks to us.

This sort of relational prayer is learned over a lifetime. But sometimes the most rudimentary prayers are the most beautiful. Sometimes when you hear someone pray for the first time, he or she shrugs and says, "That was terrible! You guys pray so much better than me." But the rawness and the truth of that person's attitude conveyed in the prayer is often the most beautiful thing you could possibly hear. And so, we gather to pray as a church every single Sunday. We gather to hear the prayers of all of the people.

When the pastor steps to the microphone and prays for us, we are also praying as one to our Father, learning in this precious

---

2. William H. Willimon, *The Service of God: Christian Work and Worship* (Nashville: Abingdon Press, 1983), 35.

moment to speak to God ourselves. We learn vocabularies, tenses, and postures with which to speak to God. We learn much about prayer when we are together because we lift our prayers together, with one person speaking on behalf of us. Each of us is in a different stage of growth, and those who are new to the Christian faith are learning new things. For them—and even the rest of us—corporate prayers are instructive, shaping each one's individual prayers with the very words being spoken on behalf of the group.

The 1989 movie *Glory* was about the fifty-fourth Massachusetts Regiment during the Civil War, a volunteer African American regiment, with a white general, fighting for the Union against the South. In the movie, the African American soldiers regularly gather at the end of the day to sing spirituals and pray. Before a particularly big battle, they also gather and take turns praying for each other. As a man who has known God all his life, the first soldier to pray, Sergeant Major Rawlins (played by Morgan Freeman), offers a beautiful prayer. The next person to pray, Private Trip (played by Denzel Washington), begins his prayer by saying, "I ain't much about no prayin', now."[3] Despite the awkwardness and the discomfort expressed by the private, the community gathers around both soldiers and affirms their prayers. That they are all praying together matters more than whether the words are uttered eloquently or awkwardly.

When we gather to pray, we come from different life situations, with different struggles, hurts, fears, and sins. But when we come to pray in a service on Sunday, we are all together in this act of prayer! And in this act of corporate prayer, we learn who

---

3. "'Glory' Quotes (1989)," Moviequotes.com, accessed March 31, 2020, https://www.moviequotes.com/s-movie/glory/.

we are and who we are meant to be; we learn how to pray, and we encourage each other through the prayers we offer.

In a worship gathering, we often have people who are talented at praying and those who may feel less eloquent. But either way, we gather to imagine something better than where we are. We fix our eyes on the heavenly realm, the one John the Revelator describes in Revelation 4–5. And we pray that as it is in the heavenly throne room, so it would be among us, God's gathered people.

After Private Trip's awkward prayer in *Glory*, his friends in the regiment, afraid for what tomorrow may hold, burst into spiritual song. They encourage each other because they learn, in prayer, that they are in this together! And they seek the help of God in their togetherness.

That's such a good way for us to move forward as a praying people, imagining who God is and what his kingdom looks like, while encouraging each other along the way. Our prayers call upon a faithful God to bring his kingdom "on earth as it is in heaven" (Matt. 6:10). As we join in saying amen—or "so be it"—we walk away having tasted heaven by acknowledging the near presence of Christ. And as we ask God for his kingdom to be on earth as it is in heaven, we recognize, as well, that we have practiced the nearness of Christ. We have had a foretaste of heaven. We, then, answer the call to be heaven bearers, owning our responsibility to make the world as we have just imagined and experienced.

But we are not alone. Not only have we acknowledged the nearness of Christ, but also our praying together gestures us toward bringing each other along. In seeing more clearly what this kingdom of God looks like, we help each other along toward a closer relationship with the risen and profoundly near Christ.

7
Receiving the Offering

● ● ●

Stanley Hauerwas writes, "One reason why we Christians argue so much about which hymn to sing, which liturgy to follow, which way to worship is that the commandments teach us to believe that bad liturgy eventually leads to bad ethics. You begin by singing some sappy, sentimental hymn, then you pray some pointless prayer, and the next thing you know you have murdered your best friend."[1]

This quote may seem extreme, until you read the story of Cain and Abel in Genesis 4. Before this account, we have the story of Cain and Abel's parents, Adam and Eve. They sinned by eating the one thing they were told not to eat. One generation later, the two brothers have grown up in the shadow of that sin, and we see how quickly sin escalates.

Abel tends the livestock, and Cain tends the land. Both know that out of their labor they are supposed to give offerings to God. The day arrives for them to give their offerings. They gather up

---

1. Stanley M. Hauerwas and William H. Willimon, *The Truth about God: The Ten Commandments in Christian Life* (Nashville: Abingdon Press, 1999), 89.

what they want to give. Abel, the one who tends the livestock, decides that God is so good, that he loves God so much, and that he understands God's goodness so intimately, that he's going to bring the best, fattest livestock he can possibly bring to God. He brings the one that has the best brisket, the finest porterhouse, the greatest T-bone—the one that would be the most delicious, and he says, "I could consume this with joy, but I choose to offer this to you, God."

On the other hand, Cain gets nervous. He thinks, "I have grains and vegetables that I have grown. They're beautiful; even organic! But if I gave away the best, would there be enough for my family to eat? The best are what my family needs to live on. I love God, but I also have to care for my family. I'll grab some of the lesser crops and bring those. I want to worship, but I have mouths to feed."

The brothers come to God to present their offerings. Abel goes first and gives his fattened animals. God is very pleased with the gift. Cain gives his half-baked, mediocre gift, and God seems to say, "That's nice. Thanks."

Cain is a little worked up, as if to say, "What's the matter? I don't even understand why he gave the best. That is irresponsible. What's the problem here?"

God responds with this fascinating line in Genesis 4:7: "If you do what is right, will you not be accepted? But if you do not do what is right, sin is crouching at your door." God seems to be saying that a mediocre offering is sinful. Instead, he means that the one who could only imagine giving a mediocre offering has sin crouching at the door, as if that person is more susceptible to sin. Abel, who can imagine that God will provide, gets no warning. But to Cain, the one who needs to pick and choose what he thinks he is able to give, God says, "Sin is crouching at your door."

Sure enough, sin is crouching at his door. Before long, out of jealousy, Cain kills his brother. He can't imagine his brother being better in the eyes of God: his brother was lavish, irresponsible. So rather than listen to the explicit call of God or understand what has pleased God, he chooses instead to eliminate his brother. In just one generation, we go from eating forbidden fruit to murder.

So, sin has a way of crouching at our door. Bad worship practices led to murdering a brother. And Stanley Hauerwas may not be so outlandish, after all.

In our society today, we find ourselves so often honestly, unconsciously, accidentally pursuing things that are not of God. We may not be in danger of sin crouching so near our doors that we murder, but the story remains clear: the way we give to God is indicative of whether sin is crouching at our door. We are pleased to bring our offerings to Apple when it provides a new iPhone or iPad. We are honored to give an offering to Chipotle, McDonald's, or the local artisanal chef who makes a delicious avocado toast. We gladly pay fees for our children to participate in activities that will qualify them for college scholarships, at the steep price of removing them from church attendance for a season. In Western culture, there is no shortage of places to spend our money. We assume that how we spend is amoral. It is not. Our spending forms the persons we are. We are shaped by our spending habits.

Several years ago, the church I pastored hosted two Ugandan families. Both families were in the United States for heart surgeries for their children, ages three and one. The surgeries were scheduled, pro bono, in Maine, and we hosted the families during the surgeries and through follow-up appointments. The families stayed with one of my staff pastors, Cheryl.

Cheryl would come to my office and tell me stories about so-called commonsense American practices that the Ugandans perceived to be crazy. According to the Ugandans' common sense, life in America was extravagant and bizarre. They called Americans "crazy mzungus." They could not believe that Americans bought food for dogs at a store and that there were entire aisles dedicated to this. Crazy mzungus. They could not believe that we had electric washing machines. Crazy mzungus. They could not believe RVs were buses, not houses. Crazy mzungus.

The idea of common sense is really a fallacy. It has far more to do with what is common in one's culture than anything to do with sense. We are shaped into what our culture calls common sense instead of inheriting and living by some cosmological truth. Common sense becomes something we throw ourselves into so that we don't have to examine ourselves. It is a defense mechanism as much as it is an explanation. When we appeal to common sense, we no longer must think about what God is doing and who God is calling us to be. We don't have to change or move; we can become comfortable. And if there is anything that is more American than comfort, I don't know what it is. We love comfort. In fact, I would dare say that we are bordering on the worship of comfort. We want to be comfortable, and there is no price too high for us to achieve it.

One of those things that comes close to our idolatry of comfort is our lust for romantic love. If there's anything in our society that we will risk our beloved comfort for, it is romantic love. This is best modeled in the movie *Say Anything*, in which John Cusack's character throws a boom box over his head and stands outside the girl's window in the rain. How cheesy is that? Yet there are people who argue that it is the most romantic movie scene ever. We will risk our comfort if we think that love is on the other side of it.

Think back to the terrible dresses you wore to go to homecoming or the horrific matching ties you wore to prom or the awful powder-blue tux you have in your wedding photo! We will do silly things if we think love is on the other side of it. These otherwise bizarre behaviors are "common sense."

When I was a child, a movie played over and over in my house was *Sister Act*, starring Whoopi Goldberg. The story was about a woman living the fast life in Reno and hiding out in a convent to escape danger. She decides to help the church by enlivening the nuns' choir. The movie played with the idea that secular songs about romantic love could, with just a tweak of your imagination, become about God. The choir becomes so famous that the church is packed weekly, and eventually, the choir sings the song "I Will Follow Him" in front of the pope.

While the movie is fun and funny, I wonder if there's something wrong with the way we talk about God if we can sing a song that is about a boyfriend and then easily remake it into a song about God. Does this not show that there is something wrong with the grammar and language we use to understand who God is? It does not end here, because there are many songs on Christian radio that are best defined as "Jesus is my boyfriend" songs. We need to rethink our conception of God and our worship practices if we include such songs in church worship.

Again, the one thing we can imagine possibly risking ourselves for today is romantic love. If we think we can have that sweet, romantic kiss under the moonlight, risk becomes imaginable. But when it comes to risking ourselves for God, we come up with all sorts of excuses.

There was a song that was popular during my high school years titled "I'm Gonna Be (500 Miles)." It was famous for its beat and its offbeat lyrics (the band is Scottish, after all). One of the lines in the song that is particularly interesting has the singer telling his beloved he will give most of the money he earns to her.[2] It's fascinating that we will empty the bank account just to show how much we love the object of our romantic desire. We even have a cultural narrative that says giving the best gifts demonstrates love. When Christmas season comes, Lexus has ads in which they place bows on $60,000 cars. Most of us would not have to work next year if we got a Lexus, because selling it would exceed an annual salary. People are giving Lexus luxury cars for Christmas gifts! But that is how you show love in our society—by giving extravagantly.

Although we rarely celebrate giving money in church to God, for whom we profess our greatest love, we celebrate many things that divert our attention from God. We revel in some bizarre things, such as the television show *House Hunters*, in which twenty-five-year-olds working as balloon-design advisers and pet-iguana trainers can somehow afford a $600,000 house! We celebrate the show *Hoarders*, which makes a spectacle of people who can't get control of their excess stuff. We elect presidents whose chief campaign strategists use the line "The economy, stupid."[3] Not justice for the poor? Not care for our widows? No. "The economy, stupid."

We listen to people on television and radio and justify their messages because they say they are Christians. Many of these Christian broadcasters say their goal is to make us rich! They say that being rich means God's blessing has come upon us. Their message, the so-called prosperity gospel, drastically contrasts with the actual message of Scripture, which says that God's blessing has already come upon us. The belief—like the message proclaimed

---

2. The Proclaimers, "I'm Gonna Be (500 Miles)," by Charlie Reid and Craig Reid, recorded 1988, track 1 on *Sunshine on Leith*, Chrysalis Records CHR 1668, 1988, vinyl LP.

3. Wikipedia, s.v. "It's the Economy, Stupid," last modified March 22, 2020, 03:52, https://en.wikipedia.org/wiki/It%27s_the_economy,_stupid.

by these broadcasters—that equates God's blessing with material wealth leads people to do silly things.

Burt Reynolds, in the movie *The End*, demonstrates the silly things people do. His character is diagnosed with a very unfortunate blood disease, and he is told he has six months left to live. Instead of living life to the fullest for the next six months, all he can imagine is the tortuous, lonely death that he's going to die. The whole movie is about him being thwarted from killing himself so he can bring about "the end" before it happens naturally. He keeps trying, and a friend keeps thwarting him. He decides there is only one way he can succeed; he swims out into the middle of the ocean, where he becomes exhausted and so eliminates any chance that anyone will save him. But then he has a vision of all that he has, all that he's been given, and how lucky he is, and he decides he wants to live. He begins swimming back, while bargaining with God:

I can never make it. Help me, Lord! Please? I promise not to try to kill myself anymore. Save me and I swear that I'll be a better father! I'll be a better man! I'll be a better everything! All I ask is, Make me a better swimmer! . . .

Oh, God, let me live and I promise to obey every one of the Ten Commandments! I shall not kill. I shall not commit adultery. I shall not—I, uh—I'll learn the Ten Commandments! And then, I'll obey every . . . one of them! Just get me back to the beach. I'll be honest in business. I promise not to sell lakeside lots unless there's a lake around! I want to see another sunrise! I want to see another sunset!

There was a mistake, God. I never really wanted to kill myself. I just wanted to get your attention! Help me make it! I'll give you 50 percent of everything I make. 50 percent, God! I want to point out that nobody gives 50 percent—I'm talking gross, God!

I think I'm gonna make it! You won't regret this, Lord! I'll obey every commandment. I'll see my parents more often. No more cheating in business (once I get rid of those nine acres in the desert), and I'm gonna start donating that 10 percent right away! I know I said 50 percent, Lord, but 10 percent to start. If you don't want your 10 percent, then don't take it. I know it was you that saved me, but it was also you that made me sick![4]

When things are tough, we get in the habit of making promises to God, but when things are going well, we assume we got there by our own hard work. We believe in our own labor and skills and often turn to God only when our work has let us down. We make promises: "I'll give you this. I'll start doing that. Please just make things right—make things comfortable again." Then, like Burt Reynolds's character, we begin to change the narrative as soon as we begin to feel comfortable again. We don't live as well in partnership with God when we're lavished with God's blessings as we do when we're desperate. But maybe God is a God of more than just our desperation.

As we mentioned earlier, it is all too easy to treat God like a genie with a lamp. Whenever we need something, when things are really bad, we only have to rub the lamp and God will appear and fix everything for us. But God is seeking so much more than this. God is seeking to be in partnership and relationship with us. Our offering is one of the best ways for us to give back to God out of what he has first given us.

The offering received at church demonstrates three theological concepts. First, it demonstrates, proclaims, testifies, that everything we have belongs to God. We have not attained stuff by our

---

4. *The End*, directed by Burt Reynolds (1978; Chicago: Olive Films, 2015), Blu-ray.

own will or work, but we have received from God blessings from the world he created. Second, we should tangibly trust God to provide. Finally, we should offer all of ourselves as an offering to God.

There's an old joke that says three men were together, and they were trying to decide how much money they should give to God. The first said, "What I do is I draw a circle in the middle of the room, and I throw it up in the air, and whatever lands in the circle, I give to God." The second one says, "That's faithless and mediocre! What I do is I draw a circle and whatever lands outside of the circle, I give to God." The third one says, "Well, I throw it up in the air and whatever God wants, God can keep."

That's not how it works, is it?

How much more generous would we be if we understood ourselves, not as receivers and spenders of money, but as stewards of God's world? How would we behave if we realized that we were to treat the things we receive like the oxygen we breathe into our lungs, inhaling and exhaling, receiving and giving, all the while trusting God? We are stewards of God's world, and what we have is not ours but God's.

This leads us to the second theological concept, that we should trust God to provide. The story of God giving manna in the desert after freeing the Israelites from slavery is instructive. The freed slaves, God's people, are wandering the desert, and every morning there is food for them to eat. They gather food, but at the end of the day, the food spoils, so they never gather more than one day's worth. God provided enough manna for each new day. We need to again trust that God will provide for us tomorrow if we trust him with our today: "Give us this day our daily bread" (Matt. 6:11, KJV).

And then finally, proceeding to the third theological concept, the liturgical act of offering during worship is the placing of ourselves on the altar. Romans 12 states that we should offer our bodies as a living sacrifice. In a world of commerce, cash, and capitalism, one way we incorrectly understand ourselves is by how much money we have. And while that's a horribly incomplete understanding of personhood, our society urges us to define ourselves in terms of monetary gain. As such, by giving up ourselves as an offering to God, we are placing our capitalist, malformed image on the altar as well. We recall one of the best-known stories of placing what one values most on an altar—the account of Abraham and his son Isaac. In faith, Abraham placed his son Isaac on an altar to be sacrificed to God, but God supplied an offering—"a ram caught in a thicket" (Gen. 22:13, KJV)—in the nick of time so Isaac could be spared. Perhaps if we were to offer God what we imagine we cannot live without, there would be a ram in the thicket for us. We may also find that as we give sacrificially to God, we will rediscover whose we are. We are not what we accumulate. We are created in the image of God to be partners with God.

There is an obscure story in the Old Testament of King Ahaz and his son King Hezekiah. Ahaz was a terrible king, perhaps the wickedest king in the history of Israel. He had stewardship of the Southern Kingdom, where Jerusalem was located. By this time, the two kingdoms had split, and of the twelve tribes of Israel, ten were ruled by their king in the Northern Kingdom, and two were ruled by their king in the Southern Kingdom. Because the Southern Kingdom contained the holy city of Jerusalem, with the temple, the two tribes composing this kingdom had the ability to worship properly. They had every opportunity to be the kingdom that pleased God.

According to the Old Testament, after becoming king of the Southern Kingdom at the age of twenty, Ahaz is confronted with Syria and the Northern Kingdom, who attempt to force the Southern Kingdom into an alliance with them against Assyria. Not wanting this alliance, Ahaz enters into conflict with the Northern Kingdom and Syria. Needing to win this war while shorthanded, Ahaz reaches out to the Assyrians—a pagan, yet powerful, people. King Ahaz makes an agreement with the Assyrian king that if the Assyrians will defeat the Northern Kingdom and Syria, they can make the Southern Kingdom an Assyrian vassal.

Assyria, predictably, sacks the Northern Kingdom and Syria, and, in return for their victory, sets up altars to foreign and false gods on every block in the city of Jerusalem. King David's city becomes a shrine to false, foreign gods, and Ahaz feels protected now because his enemies are defeated.

Sometimes in our limited imagination, we think of things such as comfort, safety, and the future, and we begin to distance God from these dreams. We sell ourselves out to comfort, and we do not see how we have shifted our allegiance from living for the kingdom of God to living our best, most comfortable lives. We struggle to even see the idolatry in this shift, because the goal in our society—our "commonsense goal"—is to be comfortable.

Ahaz is now comfortable. He has the largest army in the neighborhood watching his back! He is fully safe, yet as a practicing idolater, he is now leading his people even deeper into the worship of false gods: the Assyrians remove the worship of Yahweh from the temple and begin to decorate it with their own liturgical art and idols.

Finally, Ahaz dies. His son Hezekiah becomes the king. But unlike his father, Hezekiah has a deep desire to make things right. He gathers the Levites and priests and says, "We need to purify the land." They begin taking down altars and removing the Assyrian idols. The people begin to express a yearning to worship their God once more. They continue purifying the land until the time for worship arrives. Second Chronicles 31:1-10 tells the story:

> When all this had ended, the Israelites who were there went out to the towns of Judah, smashed the sacred stones and cut down the Asherah poles. They destroyed the high places and the altars throughout Judah and Benjamin and in Ephraim and Manasseh. After they had destroyed all of them, the Israelites returned to their own towns and to their own property.
>
> Hezekiah assigned the priests and Levites to divisions—each of them according to their duties as priests or Levites—to offer burnt offerings and fellowship offerings, to minister, to give thanks and to sing praises at the gates of the Lord's dwelling. The king contributed from his own possessions for the morning and evening burnt offerings and for the burnt offerings on the Sabbaths, at the New Moons and at the appointed festivals as written in the Law of the Lord. He ordered the people living in Jerusalem to give the portion due the priests and Levites so they could devote themselves to the Law of the Lord. As soon as the order went out, the Israelites generously gave the firstfruits of their grain, new wine, olive oil and honey and all that the fields produced. They brought a great amount, a tithe of everything. The people of Israel and Judah who lived in the towns of Judah also brought a tithe of their herds and flocks and a tithe of the holy things dedicated to the Lord their God, and they piled them in heaps. They began doing this in the third month and finished in the seventh month. When Hezekiah and his officials came and saw the heaps, they praised the Lord and blessed his people Israel.
>
> Hezekiah asked the priests and Levites about the heaps; and Azariah the chief priest, from the family of Zadok, answered, "Since the people began to bring their contributions

to the temple of the LORD, we have had enough to eat and plenty to spare, because the LORD has blessed his people, and this great amount is left over."

We hear the language of "firstfruits," or the first and best of the produce, which recalls our earlier story, that of Cain and Abel. Abel offered his first and best, his "firstfruits," and God was pleased. Here, the people bring a tithe of all they have because they want to worship God. That is their priority; it is who they yearn to be, first and foremost. They felt distanced from God, so now they are excited. They do not bring a small offering; they bring their firstfruits, and a tenth at that.

The story ends with God's blessing on them, because God is not about taking. He is not a God of contractual obligation; he does not dispense his blessings only if we place our tenth in an offering plate. He is a God who works with us and gives to us throughout our entire lives. He is a God of abundance, and he gives out of love for his people.

We give in response to God's abundance. In God's economy, the way he sees the world, he keeps giving. He doesn't stop giving when we do. He gives, receives, and gives back. This is how God wants to work with his people. It's how God imagines life to be. He gives, we give back to him, and he blesses us anew. There is manna every morning in the desert.

In this economy, we don't store up, hold back, grasp, and cling. We receive and we give back, and we find that God is always giving more than we give. What's interesting about the concept of tithing, one wildly overlooked by Christian people, is that God gives *ten times more* than people give. That's God's economy. Throughout the years, I've heard people testify that life is far more blessed when we are working with God, receiving his gifts, giving back, and finding that he supplies needs we imagined we couldn't do without. There are countless stories about people opening mailboxes and finding checks for the exact amount God called them to give. There are stories about new adventures, new relationships, and financial needs being met for those who trust in God.

I regularly find that the most joyful Christian people are those who take a risk on behalf of God and see beyond what we may label as common sense. God can do something miraculous in our lives once we say, "I'm not about to do it by myself anymore; I'm going to join God and work with him. I want to be his coconspirator." These joyful people are blessed, happy, and overwhelmingly surprised at how present and active God is in our world today. Their simple risky trust in God is enough to bring them great joy. Sometimes tangible benefits come in return; sometimes they do not. Either way, the life of faithful response often brings a fulfillment that this world, in itself, does not supply.

8
Greeting Time
• • •

Despite my intense dislike for running, I am a runner. I find that I am healthier and happier when I run regularly, even though I hate it while I am doing it. To soothe my hatred, I listen to podcasts while I run. It is like running with a friend, but there is no pressure to add anything to the conversation with the precious little oxygen I can spare. Many runners accuse me of being wrong: most people listen to music, but music often feels repetitive and does not occupy my mind enough. Podcasts engage my brain, so I forget that my lungs and legs are killing me.

Each year, I run the Beach to Beacon 10K in Cape Elizabeth, Maine. One year I forgot to download a podcast and so I was relying on the Internet. I strongly recommend visiting Cape Elizabeth, but I would also highly recommend not relying on the Internet data signal there. Service can be spotty, especially on the Beach to Beacon course.

Around mile two, my Internet quit working, so I was without podcast. I had to switch over to downloaded music on my phone. Since that is not how I usually run, I was afraid I was going to do very poorly. As I pressed on, the song "Boulevard of Broken Dreams," by the band Green Day, came on. That song is a particularly depressing song. I have a friend who suffers from depression who cannot listen to that song because he feels darkness coming over him when he hears it.

The song is about loneliness, and although I was running the Beach to Beacon, it felt appropriate, because no one was going to run 6.2 miles *for* me. I truly ran alone.

"Boulevard of Broken Dreams" encapsulates one of the real struggles of living in today's world: that while being more connected than any point in the history of the world, we are also as lonely as we have ever been. It is an anthem of a lonely generation.[1]

In the January 2012 issue of *Psychological Science*, a study out of Purdue University was published about the power of making eye contact with another person. Purdue University has over forty thousand students. One research assistant traversed a busy path of the school and addressed 428 people at random, in one of three ways:

1. met the person's eyes
2. met the subject's eyes and smiled
3. looked in the direction of the individual's eyes—but past, for example, an ear[2]

---

1. Green Day, "Boulevard of Broken Dreams," by Billie Joe Armstrong, Mike Dimt, Tré Cool, recorded September 2003, track 4 on *American Idiot*, Reprise Records 9362-48777-1, 2004, compact disc.

2. Eric D. Wesselmann, Florencia D. Cardoso, Samantha Slater, and Kipling D. Williams, "To Be Looked at as Though Air: Civil Attention Matters," *Psychological Science* 23, no. 2 (January 2012), 166-68, https://doi.org/10.1177/0956797611427921.

The director of the study, Dr. Eric D. Wesselmann, described the third approach as "looking at them as if they were air."[3]

Immediately after passing the initial researcher, another researcher would stop the subject and ask how disconnected from other people he or she felt. Those who received eye contact from the original researcher reported feeling more connected than did those who were looked past. On a campus of forty thousand people, being looked past versus being acknowledged had at least a momentary impact on the feelings of connectedness in students on campus.

Famous and wealthy, Lady Gaga is living the "dream," yet she nearly quit music. She almost walked away. She explained that she had become just an image to look at and was no longer seen as a person. Fame had eroded her personhood. She described her feelings:

> I don't like . . . just shaking people's hands . . . smiling . . . taking selfies. It feels shallow. . . . I have a lot more to offer than my image. . . .
>
> . . . I started to say no. . . . And slowly but surely, I remembered who I am.[4]

Commenting on social media and the false images people present, Lady Gaga goes on to say that instead of really communicating, "We are unconsciously communicating lies."[5]

What if she is right? What if we live in a world that is now so digital that we hide our true selves behind Facebook pages or

---

3. "Eye Contact and Social Interaction," PsyArticles.com, accessed October 27, 2017, http://www.psyarticles.com/inter-personal/social-interaction.htm.

4. Paul Schrodt, "Lady Gaga Discovered How to Be Happy When She Started Saying One Word a Lot More Often," Business Insider, last modified October 30, 2015, http://www.businessinsider.com/lady-gaga-yale-speech-2015-10.

5. Ibid.

Twitter and Instagram accounts? The problem with Facebook is that we display on it the best of our lives, and while obscuring ourselves, we also do not want to see the struggles of others. When someone rants about being upset, we think about blocking his or her page. Facebook is a false reality. We find that slowly but surely, we are erasing the truth of who we are; we are trying our best, through perfectly worded text messages or perfectly lit Instagram images, to portray ourselves as having it all together.

Lady Gaga found that she was erasing her humanity. She no longer felt human but rather was an image for picture taking, a brand to be marketed.

We are also in danger of erasing our humanity by no longer being human with each other. We have fewer outlets, forums, and communities to share our burdens. We rarely take the time to look someone else in the eye and ask how he or she is doing. Instead, we ask how a person is doing only as a matter of decorum, as we're running to our next activity, hoping the person doesn't respond with a lengthy answer. Our busyness has become an idol. We have our next place to go and our next thing to do, and we are checking off boxes on our agenda, rooted in a false reality of who we are. We are erasing our humanity as we behave this way. We are slowly becoming something we are not, in the name of an image that looks good to those too busy to notice.

Now the problem with this behavior is that it is patently un-Christian. Christianity is about a relationship with God that slows us down. We have been gifted by God's design with Sabbath, even as it has been ignored. Sabbath is the Christian discipline that invites us to work hard for six days and rest lavishly on the seventh. In that rest, we Christians gather together in worship, and part of our worship is then to experience Sabbath in community. This vitally important, baseline belief of the Christian faith is not practiced individually.

Andrea Yates is a cautionary tale. She was in the news in 2001 for drowning her own children. She testified to doing so for religious reasons: she believed God's voice and the Scriptures directed her to take this action because of the children's unruliness. She was reading the Scriptures alone and interpreting them through her own lens. Although Andrea Yates is an extreme example, afflicted with mental illness as she was, we all need to be on guard for the danger isolated worship and study can arouse. We gather together in worship, recognizing others, not only to keep our beliefs in check and make sure that we're not stepping outside of basic, orthodox beliefs but also to be an encouragement to each other. We must take holy moments to look another person in the eye and say, "God loves you, and I love you too."

Culturally, we are at a moment when we feel justified being mean on the Internet because we seem to be speaking into a void and not to people. We cannot see the pain on their faces when we hurt their feelings; we do not know a stranger's backstory in a comments section or the intent of typed words without the benefit of vocal inflections. We struggle to bring empathy to Internet interactions, because we can never look in the eyes of those reading our words. Often we feel perfectly fine writing terrible things because we don't have to see someone else's reaction. It feels good to be a cultural warrior and speak our piece.

By contrast, the Christian tradition of worship invites us to see each other face-to-face. We believe that in gathering together "in real life," we more often act in ways that bring joy to others, that lift them up and testify to them that things are going to be okay because they are in Christ. The Bible speaks over and over about the hospitality and kindness of Christian community. Hear these numerous instances that call us to community:

- "Live in harmony with one another. Do not be proud, but be willing to associate with people of low position. Do not be conceited" (Rom. 12:16).
- "How good and pleasant it is when God's people live together in unity!" (Ps. 133:1).
- "I appeal to you, brothers and sisters, in the name of our Lord Jesus Christ, that all of you agree with one another in what you say and that there be no divisions among you, but that you be perfectly united in mind and thought" (1 Cor. 1:10).
- "For where two or three gather in my name, there am I with them" (Matt. 18:20).
- "Finally, all of you, be like-minded, be sympathetic, love one another, be compassionate and humble" (1 Pet. 3:8).
- "Dear friends, since God so loved us, we also ought to love one another" (1 John 4:11).
- "And the believers were one in heart and mind. No one claimed that any of their possessions was their own, but they shared everything they had" (Acts 4:32).
- "May the God who gives endurance and encouragement give you the same attitude and mind toward each other that Christ Jesus had" (Rom. 15:5).
- "Make every effort to keep the unity of the Spirit through the bond of peace" (Eph. 4:3).
- "And let us consider how we may spur one another on toward love and good deeds, not giving up meeting together, as some are in the habit of doing, but encouraging one another—and all the more as you see the Day approaching" (Heb. 10:24-25).

These are just some of the one-liners in the Bible; we don't have space to walk through longer narratives and parables that point us to hospitable living in community as a core spiritual discipline. It is in the very DNA of the Christian faith, and the Scripture writers recognized this. As such, the apostle Paul made unity one of his major themes. I suspect his pro-unity emphasis is an indication of how difficult unity is to achieve.

Today's congregations are made up of people who voted for different political candidates, are in different tax brackets, like different sports teams, and have different personalities. All of these differences are magnified by social media, where opinions not apparent in church are often openly shared. Yet on Sunday morning, people gather up their politics, loyalties, personalities, checkbooks, and personal baggage and go to church together. The Bible argues vehemently and specifically to love one another.

Greeting time—or, in a liturgical service, passing the peace—is done as an outward expression of a very important, fundamental belief of the Christian faith—that is, whether two people agree or disagree, they still demonstrate their love for each other. We express—in the extending of handshakes or hugs—that the kingdom of God is alive in us, that we see Christ developing in our brothers and sisters, and that that is the most important thing we see in our life together. It's the job of our fellow churchgoers to help tend the garden God planted in us by demonstrating love and by wishing peace upon our lives.

The apostle Paul did this a lot in his letters. One place is in Romans 16. As you no doubt know, Romans is one of the most theologically deep books in the Bible. There are topics in Romans that can melt the mind: justification by faith, forgiveness of sins, Jewish-Gentile relations, and so on.

Why did Paul write a pastoral letter that was so theological? It may be because the Christians in Rome had some significant disagreements with each other. Perhaps some people in that church disagreed strongly with Paul and were working to correct his "incorrect" teachings. So Paul writes Romans stating why he teaches as he does. After instructing and defending, Paul gets to the end of the letter and writes the final chapter and gives greetings to everyone.

Paul greets Phoebe, Priscilla, Aquila, Epenetus, Mary, Adronicus, Junia, and others. Notice two things: Paul is greeting many people, and he is greeting both males and females. Paul understands that women have an important role in the ministry of the church. Of all people named here, some may be on Paul's side and some may be rivals. And yet Paul realizes that it's vitally important to name and recognize each person, to dignify each one's humanity and calling in Christ, whether friend or foe.

To Paul the greetings are important. Imagine being one of the people named—hard at work in the name of the gospel, struggling, maybe even exhausted—and Paul sends greetings. He recognizes you, he points you out, and he does so publicly, in front of everyone. It probably provided a charge of energy that these people needed to keep going. It gave them dignity in their work, and hopefully they pressed on.

We do not have to be the apostle Paul to give dignity to another. We don't have to be smart, famous, or a pastor. In the midst of a worship service, we can touch someone on the shoulder, look the person in the eyes, and say, "I really appreciate you." "Thank you for your smile." "Thank you for what you do with the children." Imagine if we used our energies in the church to build each other up. Instead of critiquing the band's playing or choice of song, instead of critiquing whether your child was taught correctly, instead of critiquing the appropriateness of someone else's attire, imagine, instead, if we pronounced blessings! How different would the church be if we became that sort of people?

Greeting one another in church is an ancient act of worship. It dates to the earliest Christian liturgical practices, and we can practice being shaped by Paul's writings, greeting each other, thanking each other, and speaking life to each other.

The movie *The Truman Show* is about a television director that acquires and raises a baby to adulthood on film. All of America can watch the child, Truman, grow into adulthood. His whole life is available for viewing, twenty-four hours a day, via cable. Moreover, Truman is the only person in the dark about his circumstances; all others are voyeurs, mad scientists, and actors. People in his daily life are, in fact, actors paid to evoke certain responses from him.

Truman's entire life is manipulated—the radios, the televisions, his neighbors, his wife—for the sake of TV. As he ages, Truman notices peculiarities, but he is always kind to people. By the end of the movie, when he discovers he is the object of a TV show and wants to leave, everyone around him becomes sad. The TV viewers are sad because they're going to miss Truman. The people who work on the set are sad because they're going to miss Truman's kindness. Eventually, Truman makes his escape from the world made for him into an unfamiliar world—one that is more true and real. He enters the "real world."

We Christians find ourselves part of another world as well. In the Christian faith, we strive to be a part of the kingdom of God. We want to see Christ face-to-face; we want to know him, hold him, and love him. And we believe he is coming, that we will see him again.

But the issue here—the overarching theme of this book—is that when we come to church to worship, we are practicing the kingdom of God. Everything we do is practice for when it becomes our full reality, when we see Christ face-to-face. The worship service is not just an hour we give to God and say, "All right, now bless me, because I've given you what is yours." We worship—do the acts of worship—to shape the very core of who we are, to ready us for heaven. Therefore, we practice together. This practice is intended not just for a faraway time and a faraway future kingdom but for today. It begins to shape and change us now so that as we leave the worship service, we can live out the reality of the kingdom and be its agents in the world.

We thus practice the act of greeting so that we can show the love of Christ to others, both inside and outside the church. We practice looking each other in the eye, smiling, building each other up, and telling people that the possibility of peace is real when Christ is in our lives. We do these things so that we can be shaped and formed into kingdom citizens now, not just hoping we can live like Christ someday. When we worship, we glorify God, but we also practice in order to become shaped in the image of God.

Greeting time is specifically practice, reflection, and development. Although the world is attempting to form us into lonely people, this practice of worship is making us into a different sort of people, formed by a different sort of kingdom: a generous people, a kind people. And the hope and prayer is that as we worship together, receive the blessing, and go out into the world, our practice will have made us a little more like Christ. And so when we finally meet Christ in his fullness, we will behave accordingly.

Because as we worship, we are in the presence of Christ now, his presence and our acts of worship are helping us become a certain kind of people that will be the same when we see the kingdom in its fullness. We can be clothed in kingdom values now.

In my tradition, Wesleyan-Arminianism, we call that holiness. We believe that who we will be when we are face-to-face with Christ is who we can be now in this world. Attending weekly worship, making that *the* priority of our schedules, and participating in liturgical acts as simple as shaking hands and passing the peace shape us into becoming the people we will be when we enter the kingdom that Christ has prepared for us in its fullness.

9
Sermon

• • •

Christ the King Sunday became part of the Christian calendar in 1925—just under a hundred years ago. Pope Pius XI instituted this feast after looking across the world and observing that it was growing more secular. He urged us to remember that Christ is the King, not governments, not politics, not culture, not any other activities. He wanted to remind us in an annual feast that Christ is the King of our lives and that the incredibleness of his sacrifice on the cross designated him King of the world. And so now there is a celebration and a reminder that Christ is the King, as well as a realization that we have lost sight of that.

Pius XI's declaration was specifically to Catholics and Christians, in whom he observed an unacceptable secularization. We are now two or three generations removed from the extreme individualism of modernism, but our churches still need to be called away from secular individualism and to kingdom ethics and living.

One of the church's remedies to individualism is the sermon. Often parishioners will approach their pastor after a sermon and declare, "It was as if you were preaching directly to me!" Yet most pastors will admit that is not the case. The sermon is always a gift given to the entire congregation; it is the fruit of the pastor's labor for the week. The sermon is never meant to be a grenade lobbed at a person wallowing in sin. Rather, the sermon is the fruit of prayer, study, visitation, and conversation; it is the product of wrestling with God, mourning with the sorrowful, studying commentaries and other resources, and living within a particular community. Sermons emerge out of the pastoral life and vocation as much as they are constructed by the direct labor of the pastor. The sermon is what we need to hear (preacher included). It should be directed toward developing the people we are going to be.

It is often taken for granted that the sermon is central to why we go to church, especially in evangelical circles. But our idea of a sermon today is fairly modern. A twenty-to-thirty-five-minute sermon is only about five hundred years old. If we attend a Catholic Mass, as Protestants, we would likely be surprised by the brevity of the homily. The sermon as we know it today is a by-product of the sixteenth-century Protestant Reformation, which began in 1517 when Martin Luther nailed his Ninety-Five Theses to the door of the Castle Church in Wittenberg, Germany.

Although the Catholic Church did not agree with the critique of its practices highlighted in Luther's Ninety-Five Theses, a groundswell of people did. So eventually a schism erupted.[1] This beginning of the Protestant stream of the Christian religion was

---

1. Schism was not Martin Luther's intent. In fact, scholars believe that Luther expected his Ninety-Five Theses to be more or less ignored. Even when it gained steam, he did not yearn for schism. It is also important to note that this is not the first schism in the history of the church, since there was a similarly painful and large schism in 1054 between the Eastern Orthodox Church and the Roman Catholic Church (in the West), known as the Great Schism.

soon followed by the intense and often violent conflict between Catholics and Protestants.

Wanting desperately to defend their side, the Protestants began preaching longer sermons. And not only did they want to defend what they believed, but they also wanted to restore to laypeople access to Scripture, theology, and devotion. They believed that salvation through Jesus Christ was a decisive step in which people must place their trust in God and not just rely on someone else telling them that God had saved them. The Protestants, thus, wanted to place belief in the actual minds of people within the church. They didn't want people to believe something was true just because the church said so; they wanted people to truly believe something because they owned it in their hearts and lives. So the sermons got longer because they were opportunities for instruction.

Prior to the late Middle Ages and the Reformation, sermons were often short and called homilies.[2] A homily was frequently just a quick retelling of the Scripture that was read that day. What was really important was the reading of Scripture and the taking of Communion. For fifteen hundred years, that's what Christian worship looked like: Word and Table. Every time Christians gathered for worship, they would read Scripture and receive Communion.

The practice of proclaiming, telling, evoking, and describing the Word of God as we do today is part of our Protestant heritage. Clearly, there is a benefit to this method: through this approach, people come to understand and believe and are invited into lay ministry (the "priesthood of all believers"). However, there is something to be said for the earlier model of reading Scripture,

---

2. There were preachers in earlier times who preached rich, lengthy sermons such as Augustine, Origen, and Chrysostom. There were also sporadic revivals of preaching. Often, though, the highlight of Christian worship gatherings was the Eucharist, not the sermon.

sharing some reflections, and centering our gathering on the Table of our Lord. My hope is that we can move forward by making Word and Table the central rhythm of Christian worship.

Does preaching, then, matter to our contemporary Christian life? One objection that we hear is that preachers can be a little boring. I know that I have bored plenty of people in my time. There is a caricature of the pastor as an old, boring person who rambles on and on. One of my favorite characters is Rev. Lovejoy of *The Simpsons*. In an episode, Homer falls asleep and then yells, and the preacher says, "Well, I seem to have lost my place, so I'll start over. Our sermon today is on constancy. . . ." And then the whole congregation falls asleep. When Rev. Lovejoy finishes, the Simpsons go home and start pulling off their clothes the moment they walk in the door. Marge, the mom, says, "Hey, calm down! You're wrinkling your church clothes." Homer responds, "Who cares? This is the best part of the week!" Lisa says, "It's the longest possible time before more church!"[3]

There are also prevailing narratives in our culture that church is for perfect people, boring people: "I am too busy for church," "It's something Mom makes me do," or "I'm thirty years old; I put in my time when I was a kid." The reasons continue: "I want to sleep in." "I want to watch the game." "I have to get ready for the game." The excuses people use for not wanting to come to church, especially to avoid listening to the sermon, can be unbelievable.

But the sermon needs to move beyond simple entertainment. I say this as someone who has taught homiletics, and I always told my students that their sermons must be two things: (1) exegetical,

---

3. Steven Dean Moore, dir., *The Simpsons*, season 8, episode 22, "In Marge We Trust," aired April 27, 1997, on Fox.

wrestling closely with the text, and (2) interesting. A sermon that is not listened to automatically mitigates its impact.

It may be helpful to understand how Jesus's great sermon, the Sermon on the Mount, functioned. Those words are difficult, and we are still unsure how to wade into those deep waters two thousand years later. We can begin by weighing Jesus's words against the cultural mindset that says, "You are perfect the way you are. You are great." Self-esteem, which is a good notion, has gotten out of control. Loving yourself has morphed into serving yourself.

The self-esteem movement has been perpetuated by pop music. There are many songs that make this point, but singer Katy Perry is especially instructive. Katy Perry, a pastor's child, grew up in the church and at first even tried to break into Christian music. Katy Perry has become an icon of the "You are just so great!" mindset. This is the theme in her song "Firework," which tells listeners that when they are feeling vulnerable, they must set off their inner spark so they can light up the sky, because they are really fireworks that everyone should see.[4]

These lyrics are quintessential "self-esteem movement" concepts. The self-esteem movement is a personal matter to me because it became very influential when I was growing up in the 1980s. Self-esteem was first discussed by the psychologist and philosopher William James in the late nineteenth century. James wondered about the gap between people's opinions of themselves and objective reality. Some people assess themselves higher than they actually are, and others assess themselves lower than they are. James analyzed this gap through the lens of self-esteem, which he defined

---

4. Katy Perry, vocalist, "Firework," by Katy Perry, Ester Dean, Mikkel S. Eriksen, Tor Erik Hermansen, and Sandy Wilhelm, released 2010, track 4 on *Teenage Dream*, Capital Records 509996 84601 1 2, 2010, vinyl LP.

as "success divided by pretensions." To feel better about oneself, one must increase the numerator (i.e., have more success) or decrease the denominator (i.e., not be bound by so many pretensions). A person with no pretensions does not need much success to have strong self-esteem, and a person who has been very successful may not feel it if he or she wrestles with many internal pretensions. Thus the criteria by which we judge ourselves matters as much in our self-assessment and self-esteem as what we actually are and do.[5]

I was born in 1981, and I can remember times when I got only a ribbon for participating when I was a loser and other times when I received a trophy for winning first or second place. As I got older, trophies, not ribbons, were given out just for showing up.

Ben Stiller starred in the movie *Meet the Fockers*, which demonstrated the rise of child rearing and parenting based on self-esteem building. His character's father, played by Dustin Hoffman, maintained a wall in his house where he proudly displayed the robust mediocrity of his son's adolescence. It contained participation ribbons, ninth-place trophies for finishing competitions, and other evidence that his son was never the best but was at least involved.

Good news is a beautiful thing. People deserve to know they are worthwhile. But in the self-esteem era, we believe that our value comes from within. People simply have to discover the best part of themselves, mine it, and display it. When people find the best of themselves that they can possibly produce, that's when they will be fully actualized.

---

5. William James, "The Consciousness of Self," chap. 10 of *The Principles of Psychology* (1890), Classics in the History of Psychology, accessed April 29, 2020, https://psychclassics.yorku.ca/James/Principles/prin10.htm.

Now I am not against self-esteem. In fact, because of the emphasis on self-esteem during my childhood, when I take a StrengthsFinder assessment, usually "self-assurance" is my number two strength. Self-esteem is an important quality because it gives people a good feeling. Our potential often is linked, in some way or another, to how we feel about ourselves. But we are increasingly losing the Christian value that Christ is the one who is at work remaking us; he is the one who is making us holy. The goal we are called to pursue is to become more like Christ, not more like the "best I can be." The Christian life is not a journey to self-actualization from within. It is, rather, the glorifying of the God who yearns to dwell with and within us.

If you turn on Christian radio or television, you will hear pastor after pastor preaching a shallow gospel: "God loves you so much that he'll give you the desires of your heart! He sees good in you and wants you to be your best!" There is very little "popular" preaching of the gospel of repentance, which declares that God wants to come in us and work with us to remove sin and help us to become holy and Christlike. God loves us as we are, yes, but he wants to work in us so that sin no longer reigns in us. Then we can become how we were designed to be from the beginning.

The self-actualization message has become so predominant in popular culture and Christian circles that people are beginning to leave the church. Yes, God loves us just the way we are, but, like a potter's project, we are not finished yet. The good in the world today that is going to come from us is the work that God the Father will do as enacted through the death and resurrection of Christ and realized through the Holy Spirit infilling us.[6] This is

---

6. Samuel M. Powell, *Discovering Our Christian Faith: An Introduction to Theology* (Kansas City: Beacon Hill Press of Kansas City, 2008), 324.

so radically different from the "pop-psychology Christianity" that people are increasingly digesting.

In an era of mediocre thematic preaching, it is instructive to digest Jesus's preaching: "Repent, for the kingdom of heaven has come near" (Matt. 4:17). This is the core message of Matthew's gospel whenever Jesus is speaking: "Repent!"

Defining repentance is important, because we have changed the definition to mean telling God we are sorry. But that misses what the word "repentance" really means. Repentance means walking in one direction, realizing it's the wrong direction, and then turning 180 degrees to begin walking in the other direction. That's much different from what the misguided preacher said: "Repent and turn your life around 360 degrees to God!" For those of you who know geometry, that's not good!

Repentance is the recognition, through God's grace, that God is speaking to us and inviting us to change the direction in which we are going and to go in his direction instead. Repenting is about turning from ourselves, that is, from satisfying our needs and our wants, and turning to God and giving him our lives, our desires, our imaginations—our everything.

We repent because Christ has become real to us. We recognize that the living Christ is calling us, loves us, and wants to be in relationship with us. We repent as a response to the Son of God, who inaugurated the kingdom of God on earth, who has died for our sins so that we can live life more abundantly, and who invites us into kingdom citizenship now.

Jesus's message of repentance is unlike the message of self-esteem. His message says, "Hey, you are loved, but you're not living out the purpose for which you were designed. Why don't you live according to your design? You were designed to be in relationship with God, to be like God—holy, sinless, whole—as I am."

Sylvester Stallone's character Rocky, the boxer from Philadelphia, knew how to preach an excellent repentance sermon. In the movie *Rocky IV*, Rocky fights Drago in Russia during the Cold War, and he beats the big blond Russian. The ring announcer puts a microphone in front of Rocky, and Rocky begins to preach a message of repentance—of all things—to the Russian people. He tells them that he has noticed a change in attitude between him and the Russian spectators. Before the fight there was animosity, but during it, he and the people changed for the better in their attitude toward each other. So if he and the spectators can change, so can everyone else. His message was, "If I can change, so can everyone."[7]

I find it pretty hard to imagine kids in Russia changing their minds about America in the mid-1980s because of a boxing match. Yet Rocky takes the moment to invite the people to repent: "If I can change, you can too."

This theme is at the heart of preaching today as well. Against all odds, the love of God found the preacher and invited him or her to repent. The preacher is then called out from the people of God. He or she is not better or different from the hearers. Now, he or she declares the stories of God in Scripture backed with the testimony, "If I can change—repent—you can too. Repent!"

The preacher has the task of evoking and inspiring what God's movement in the world looks like. He or she calls the people to join God's movement in the world, living out kingdom values, ethics, and love. Then the people, with the prayerful help of God, must respond by deciding whether they will follow God's call to repentance. If the world does not look like heaven, we must be

---

7. See *Rocky IV*, directed by Sylvester Stallone (1985; Los Angeles: Twentieth Century Fox, 2014), Blu-ray.

open continually to God's call to repentance so that he can usher in the kingdom through us!

After Jesus begins preaching on repentance, he delivers the Sermon on the Mount. The words that Jesus preaches are seemingly hard. Remember, Jesus is speaking on a mountainside to people who have been so moved by his message, his grace, and his call to repentance that they have chosen to follow him. These are not unbelievers; they are Jesus's followers, just like folks in our sanctuaries today. In spite of this, Jesus preaches to them seemingly hard words about the lifestyle following repentance.

Earlier, when Jesus begins preaching repentance, he says, "Repent, for the kingdom of heaven has come near" (Matt. 4:17). When he says "the kingdom of heaven has come near," he means that the King is present—therefore, the kingdom is near! Thus because the King is present with us when we gather together, the kingdom of heaven is also near. Jesus preaches about a lifestyle that the kingdom of heaven urges us to live into and, subsequently, live out. Here are some of the things that he says, just for a refresher. Keep in mind that repentance is the implicit background of these words, which, though seemingly hard, begin with the Beatitudes, or blessings. The Sermon on the Mount envisions the lifestyle we turn to when we repent—a lifestyle made possible with God's help.

> Blessed are the poor in spirit,
>> for theirs is the kingdom of heaven.
> Blessed are those who mourn,
>> for they will be comforted.
> Blessed are the meek,
>> for they will inherit the earth.
> Blessed are those who hunger and thirst for righteousness,
>> for they will be filled.
> Blessed are the merciful,

>   for they will be shown mercy.
> Blessed are the pure in heart,
>   for they will see God.
> Blessed are the peacemakers,
>   for they will be called children of God.
> Blessed are those who are persecuted because of righteousness,
>   for theirs is the kingdom of heaven.
>
> Blessed are you when people insult you, persecute you and falsely say all kinds of evil against you because of me. Rejoice and be glad, for great is your reward in heaven, for in the same way they persecuted the prophets who were before you. (5:3-11)

None of these "blessed" characteristics are those that we value in American culture today. Nobody is telling us on TV shows, on radio shows, on podcasts, or in music, "You ought to get persecuted; that would be cool." Or "Hey, you know, the trait you should really try out is meekness." Quite the opposite! We are told repeatedly, "Win at all costs. Win, win, win." Jesus is painting a different, countercultural picture.

What about these words in Jesus's sermon?

> You have heard that it was said to the people long ago, "You shall not murder, and anyone who murders will be subject to judgment." But I tell you that anyone who is angry with a brother or sister will be subject to judgment. Again, anyone who says to a brother or sister, "Raca," is answerable to the court. And anyone who says, "You fool!" will be in danger of the fire of hell. (Vv. 21-22)

Or what about these?

> You have heard that it was said, "Eye for eye, and tooth for tooth." But I tell you, do not resist an evil person. If anyone slaps you on the right cheek, turn to him the other cheek also.

And if someone wants to sue you and take your shirt, hand over your coat as well. If anyone forces you to go one mile, go with them two miles. Give to the one who asks you, and do not turn away from the one who wants to borrow from you.

You have heard that it was said, "Love your neighbor and hate your enemy." But I tell you, love your enemies and pray for those who persecute you, that you may be children of your Father in heaven. He causes his sun to rise on the evil and the good, and sends rain on the righteous and the unrighteous. If you love those who love you, what reward will you get? Are not even the tax collectors doing that? And if you greet only your own people, what are you doing more than others? Do not even pagans do that? Be perfect, therefore, as your heavenly Father is perfect.

Be careful not to practice your righteousness in front of others to be seen by them. If you do, you will have no reward from your Father in heaven.

So when you give to the needy, do not announce it with trumpets, as the hypocrites do in the synagogues and on the streets, to be honored by others. Truly I tell you, they have received their reward in full. But when you give to the needy, do not let your left hand know what your right hand is doing, so that your giving may be in secret. Then your Father, who sees what is done in secret, will reward you. (V. 38–6:4)

Do you hear how countercultural the sermon is? Even in Jesus's time, this was countercultural, but it has become even more countercultural to us today. Influenced by the media we consume, during the free time we have, and in the relationships we form, we try to win, to get ahead; we try to build a kingdom where we rule so that others can see our greatness and worship before us! We are taught that we are primarily consumers and that we should live our lives to consume as much as possible in order to find joy.

That is an empty promise, and we should repent of this consumerist gospel.

Jesus is saying that as long as the kingdom of heaven is near, let's behave as citizens of this kingdom, not consumers. In the kingdom of heaven, there is peace, grace, kindness, helpfulness, restoration, and hope. Jesus is inviting us to live into these values in very tangible ways now rather than live out the "I'm going to get what's coming to me" values of consumerism.

The problem with the "self-esteem Christianity" preached to us today is that its theological underpinning is more closely related to "moral therapeutic deism" than it is to the message of Jesus Christ. To define our terms, "moral" refers to doing good things, "therapeutic" refers to God taking care of us and making us feel good about ourselves, and "deism" refers to God not actually being active in our world today—that is, he's off in a distant place. With deism, God is like a bowler who lets go of the bowling ball and hopes that it knocks over all ten pins. Good luck on the other side, the deity says, as he releases his hand from his work as soon as he creates it.

Moral therapeutic deism is thus a theology of a distant God who's not involved in our world today and who wants us to do nice things so that we can feel good about ourselves. That is the predominant religion in present-day America.

Maybe that's why when we read the Sermon on the Mount today, words that should have been forming followers of the original Preacher for two thousand years now still sound foreign to us. And so, we wonder the following:

How do we even live like that?

How do we even begin to act like that?

How do we live into that?

Jesus surely must have been speaking metaphorically, right? He couldn't have been serious, that we should take a punch to one side of the face and then turn so that our opponent can strike us on the other side, too—who would *do* that? That doesn't even make sense!

So often when we hear the words of Jesus, we often want to pick and choose what works for us in the moment. We celebrate a truncated canon that we ourselves have edited. We do not always want to live into the fullness of the message Jesus preaches. Instead, we should listen anew and examine our lives in the light of Jesus's words addressed to those who are declared citizens of the kingdom. We should take seriously what he is saying and then live it out, confident that we can do so with God's help.

When we gather in church, we should expect that sometimes a sermon will step on our toes—that sometimes no matter how holy we think we are, no matter how many things we think we are getting right, the sermon will speak to us and cause us to recognize that we have fallen short. Sometimes the sermon or the reading of Scripture should seem as if it's aimed right at our hearts, calling us out.

Most Sunday's when I get up and preach, I have already been whacked around during the week by the Scripture about which I am going to speak. Rarely do I come upon a Scripture for the week and say, "Well, I've got that one nailed. I can't wait to get everyone else in line with it too!" Rather, the more I come into contact with the Scriptures, the more I recognize how great my shortfall is. I need more grace to keep pulling me in the direction of the kingdom of God, which is alive and well and moving among us. I need this Christ, who was and is alive, who wants to be seen and known, who desires to grab hold of us, and who is present among us.

That's what good preaching is: a reminder of what the kingdom of God looks like, that it is at hand, and that through grace, we can be more and more like Christ. The "uplifting" moment of the sermon should be rooted in the gospel of the kingdom. The gospel should speak so loud as to say, "It doesn't matter how far gone you've been this week, because God is still calling you. And next week, through the transformative grace of God that keeps coming to you, you can look more like Christ. Grace keeps calling for more of you, keeps grabbing hold of your heart, imagination, and personality in new ways, week after week, as the Scriptures are being read. As the story of God is being talked about, you are invited to live into the call of who God is."

> Therefore everyone who hears these words of mine and puts them into practice is like a wise man who built his house on the rock. The rain came down, the streams rose, and the winds blew and beat against that house; yet it did not fall, because it had its foundation on the rock. But everyone who hears these words of mine and does not put them into practice is like a foolish man who built his house on sand. The rain came down, the streams rose, and the winds blew and beat against that house, and it fell with a great crash. (Matt. 7:24-27)

I know myself well enough to know I'm not in control of anything. I'm not any more special than anyone else. I'm not going to pretend I'm a firework who can shoot across the sky. The more I try to build up my own kingdom, the more the pressures of the world, my struggles, my inadequacies—the waters and the winds, the streams that rise—come, whether or not I think I am excellent. But I also know this: the more that I hand myself, my personality, my personhood, my life to Christ and who he is and what he's done, the more I recognize the winds and waves of life, the more I see that I end up okay on the other side. Then I don't need a Katy Perry song to tell me that I'm okay.

Because I *am* okay. Christ is as solid a rock as this world has ever known, and even when I feel beat down, inadequate, not special, depressed, sad, and hurt, Christ is there for me to lean on.

It's not always fun or easy to submit to Jesus Christ. But we have the Holy Spirit to help and enable us, and we will always find, on the other side of the struggle, that Jesus is good. He has our best interests in mind, and he's drawing us toward a future that is indescribably good. One day we will sit face-to-face with him, and all of the times we have been pierced by a sermon and felt "Oh, I do *not* want to do that! I do not want to be that!" it will have all been worth it. When we gaze on him and see him face-to-face, we will understand how simple and shallow the things we have had to put behind us were, and how great, majestic, and wonderful he is. And it will all have been worth it then.

The weekly sermon should echo with Jesus's preaching. It should paint a vivid picture of the kingdom of God for its hearers. The sermon should declare that the kingdom of God is at hand. The sermon should declare that by grace, we have been offered citizenship to this kingdom. And the sermon should invite the hearers to live as full citizens today, tomorrow, and forever.

10
Response
• • •

In springtime, during my college years, I arranged a weekend for my girlfriend to visit me at college. She drove with other friends from high school to meet me. They came from Milwaukee to Bourbonnais, Illinois. Everyone, but my girlfriend, Charryse, knew I was going to ask her to marry me. After a Saturday with friends, we went to a local park. Our group walked to the back of the park where there was a romantic bridge over a river. At my signal, everyone walked away, leaving just Charryse and me.

I began trying to segue into the conversation:
"You look beautiful tonight."
"Thanks."
"I have loved dating you the last three years."
"Yeah."
"I look forward to spending the rest of my life with you."
"Yeah, that'll be good."

Despite my efforts, Charryse was so focused on the beauty of the night and the river that she did not even notice that all our friends had left and that I was trying to ask her to marry me. In my mind, I had set everything up perfectly, but she was not even aware that I expected a response from her.

Eventually, I just bluntly called her. She looked at me and saw everything—that we were alone, that we were in a romantic spot, that I had a small velvet box in my hand. I dropped to a knee and asked her to marry me. She cried and screamed, "Yes!"

She was prepared to respond to me, but she had not recognized in my simple questions that I was pushing toward something. I had to grab her attention more fully and point her in the right direction. When she saw, she saw.

I wonder if the same thing may be happening in worship services. Preachers can effectively ask rhetorical questions, teach the text faithfully, and engage the heart of the congregation, but they do not provide space to respond to the service. When a service is being planned or sermon being written, careful attention should be given to how the people will be able to respond. Pastors and laypeople alike pray that the Spirit would move people from sin or complacency, so the church must give hearers a chance to tangibly respond. If they are moved by the Spirit and are given no chance to respond, they will likely be as frustrated as me waiting for my girlfriend's response to my proposal. If the moment is not captured, it is likely lost.

There are many ways to create response. Once, I was talking about the body of Christ fitting together, how each part is important. Through the whole sermon I placed my five-year-old daughter at a table in the front and had her play with large Duplo blocks. I told her to build a tall "Rapunzel" tower, tear it down, and build it again and to continue building and tearing down until the end of my sermon. She was amazing and had the entire congregation transfixed. I invited everyone to come forward and take a block home and display it as a reminder that as a single Duplo block, a person may not feel very useful, but when he or she remembers being part of a set scattered across the city, he or she and others become, together, a strong tower—a full body.

Another time, at Easter, I built a small tomb in the front of the sanctuary. I preached on the resurrection and asked if we still believed in the power of the resurrection. I asked the congregation if they were praying for people who seemed to be lost causes—people who struck them as fully dead to Christ. I asked if they would write those persons' names on pieces of paper and place them in the tomb to see if God would raise the seemingly dead back to life.

Many people responded with names. Would you believe that the next week a lady came up to me and introduced me to a friend? She had a shocked look on her face as she was making the introduction. She then blurted out, "This is whose name I put in the tomb last week. She came the next week, pastor!" Eight months later, this friend was baptized. Giving people the opportunity to respond before they leave is a powerful tool of discipleship.

In my current church, I followed an extended interim pastor. He preached an effective casual sermon with a strong response. He talked about the mechanics of rowing a boat—about how all rowers must coordinate their rowing to move. Displaying a wooden oar, he then said that if the church was going to function well, everyone had to row in the same direction. The invitation was specific: set aside pet projects, personal agendas, and the "way we have always done things," and work together for the good of the kingdom. He asked the congregation if they were willing to row in the same direction. If so, using the nice pens he had set next to the oar, they could come and sign the oar as a public declaration that they were in this together. They would thus be recognizing that if they decided to row in different directions, they would be affecting more than themselves as individuals.

That moment deeply changed the DNA of the church. People were asked to respond, and it changed the culture.

In the denomination I pastor, there is a robust history of praying at the altar after the sermon. This is an excellent means of response. However, there are three drawbacks to this methodology: (1) It leads the preacher to preach toward a crisis week after week. Not every sermon needs to be a crisis. (2) It can lead a congregation to think that going to the altar is embarrassing. I recall this feeling distinctly in my teen years. People who went to the altar had something wrong with them. People were more inclined to just sort out problems in private. This led to a privatized, individualized faith. (3) This methodology leads the pastor to often understand his or her effectiveness as a preacher and pastor by how lined the altars are at the end of the service. This is nonsense, but the pastor may begin to manipulate sermons with heavy emotionalism just for the sake of validating his or her ministry with altar responses. The allure of success for pastors is intoxicating, and the altar is too important a place to mix their egos up in it.

As such, the altar as a prayer rail may best be used as a form of response among many. Be creative! Use the altar as a holy place for responsive prayer, but do not lazily become married to it as the only way to respond. Think creatively about what you, as the preacher, want your people to walk away with. What is the key point? Fashion, with intention, a response directing them toward that action, theology, behavior, or ethic.

In the history of the Christian church, well before the American Holiness Movement that shaped my church's tradition, the most common response to the Word was the Table. In 1 Corinthians 11, where Paul is teaching proper Communion ethics, he uses the phrase "when you come together" five times in the directive (vv. 17-20, 33-34, ESV). The assumption about the earliest churches, mentioned in Scripture, is that they were celebrating the Lord's Table every time they gathered together. They may not have done it well, as exhibited in the Corinthian church, but the Lord's Table was a central part of their worship gathering. The Lord's Table, Communion, Eucharist—however it is referenced—will be explored in the next chapter as the sacrament and response par excellence in the church's worship gatherings.

In the meantime, whether you serve Communion, open the altar for prayer, have the congregation stand and sing, or orchestrate a creative response, the service should be headed somewhere, and it should make clear to the hearers how they can respond to the message.

As mentioned earlier, while running, I began listening to podcasts and have, over the years, become a podcast aficionado. To share this interest, I try to alert my wife to good podcasts that we can discuss as a couple. One that intrigued me was *S-Town*. It is the story of an Alabama man, John B. McLemore, who is convinced that the identity of a murderer is an open secret and that the politics of his town, Woodstock, allows the man to live free of conviction.

An NPR reporter travels to Woodstock to see if such an accusation is true. The reporter, Brian Reed, discovers that McLemore's accusations are false, but he becomes fascinated with McLemore himself. McLemore is depressive but captivating. He is intelligent but susceptible to conspiracy theories. He cusses, he rants, and he speculates. He has unusual hobbies such as scanning the Internet for climate conspiracies and restoring old clocks.

One of the predominant town rumors is that despite his humble lifestyle, unkempt look, and lack of a will and testament, he has significant resources, including buried gold. There are many people who have an interest in this gold, and McLemore never confirms its location or existence.

To the shock of everyone, especially Brian Reed, McLemore commits suicide during the production of the podcast. He takes cyanide, which causes a painful death. Immediately, curious parties inquire about the gold. Some distant relatives hire attorneys. McLemore's mentee breaks into his property. Friends speculate about McLemore's wealth, intentions, and meticulous plans.

But the podcast ends without anyone striking it rich. The wealth appears to be buried or carefully moved. The listener never finds out what happened to the treasure. For my wife, the intrigue was enough to make her hate the podcast. She felt she wasted her time and that she was left hanging. She wanted a conclusion.

I wonder if preachers often leave worshippers hanging. Worship plans attempt to develop a compelling narrative: songs that match the sermon theme, carefully crafted readings, and a well-thought-out sermon, complete with hooks. But do we intentionally create space for the people to respond to the sermon, or do we hope that appealing to their intellect will cultivate change? Chances are a tangible response is more likely to encourage people to live out the narrative of the service than just letting them leave and "think about it" ever will.

The following chapter outlines the most classic form of Christian response: moving from Word to Table. Not every gathering demands re-creating what is already done. The early Christians longed to be at the Table Christ prepared for them. Recapturing that desire today would do the church well and would give people a regular chance to respond to the message by standing and responding to the grace given through Jesus Christ, our Lord.

11
Sacrament

• • •

The Church of the Nazarene, the denomination where I pastor, recognizes two sacraments—baptism and Communion. Sacraments are defined as outward, visible signs of inward grace, which Jesus Christ himself instituted. Both of these sacraments are meant to be a response: a response to the grace of God given, a response to the message preached, and a response to hearing what God is saying and seeing what God is doing.

Interestingly enough, I interviewed seventeen people in my congregation to hear and listen to their thoughts on the sacraments. Their responses were typical responses from those within evangelical churches like my own.

I asked, for example, "How many times do you think someone should be baptized?" Only one person said, "Once." The usual response was, "A lot of times people kind of fall away from their baptism and spend a season in sin, and if they want to come back and be baptized again, I don't see a problem with that." That is a reasonable answer. There is not necessarily something wrong with that, until you search the creeds and see that there is one baptism.[1] So what has happened between this affirmation of the traditional, historic faith and today's idea that says, "Well, I mean, if you've had a meaningful reconnection with God, then maybe you should have another baptism"?

Now may be a good time in the history of our church for us to have a widespread renewal of sacramental thinking. Although several churches and leaders are already moving in this direction, more participation is needed. This is especially so because the sacraments, as we've observed, are acts that Jesus himself instituted—and that should be more than enough encouragement to be part of this renewal! Some may argue that this is just something Catholics do. But it's not! Just as Catholics and other Christian churches belong to the history of Christ's movement in the world, so do we. And as a church that is a legitimate part of this movement, maybe we ought to do the legitimate things Jesus did.

I also asked my church people—and again, this is just a sampling of multiple generations, male and female, recent members and longtime members—"How often should we have Communion?" And again, only one or two people said, "Every week!" A lot of people said, "I think we do it too often." Most people said, "I think once a month is about right." This response was typical and in accord with what I experienced in evangelical churches across America. Many evangelicals think there is a clear line of "enough." The answer, for many, is between once a month and once every three months. The reason given behind this typical response is, "I do not want to do it so often that it loses its meaning." Once again this is a reasonable, well-thought-out, grounded-in-ex-

---

1. The Nicene Creed reads, "We acknowledge one baptism for the forgiveness of sins." *Book of Common Prayer* (New York: Church Hymnal Corporation, 1979), 359.

perience answer. There's nothing inherently wrong with any of the answers. It is interesting to hear what people think about how we are engaging in worship.[2]

In accord with the previous chapter, I make sure every week to provide for some sort of response. Having an opportunity for our bodies to respond physically to the Word is vital to our formation. Rather than just checking off boxes in our minds, we want our physical bodies to respond to the preaching of the gospel; we want to take a stand by literally standing and moving in the direction of God.

But again, historically the church as a whole, until recently, has practiced weekly Communion. And so now scholars in several Protestant churches are asking, "What has happened? Why is it that we no longer receive Communion every week?"

There are some cynics who observe that music has become the sacrament of choice of many Protestants. Think about it: What if a pastor told a congregation that because he or she fears music could lose its meaning because of its frequent use, the church will now sing just once a month to ensure music stays special? There would be a riot!

But yet, we have taken the meal that Jesus himself handed to his followers and have begun to evaluate it on the basis of what we feel. And whether or not *we* feel something is exactly how *we* judge its importance. And so, we have taken this idea of sacrament, the gift that Christ himself instituted and gave to the church, in both baptism and Communion, and we have said, "Our feeling is king. What we feel, what we experience, validates or invalidates it."

---

2. Full disclosure: my church has Communion nearly every week. A segment of the population loves receiving Communion weekly, and another segment thinks it is excessive. I have great respect for those in both camps.

And yet, this is a bizarre way to behave, because so much about life—our personalities, our routines, and so on—are shaped and designed after the mundane. Life is often routine and boring. If we really had to sit down and describe who we are and what we do, we would have to refer to mundane moments to describe it. "I get up in the morning, go to work, eat lunch, go home, talk to my children, tuck them into bed, converse with my spouse, watch our DVR shows, and go to bed." It's mundane and boring, and yet it's so formative to our story and who we are. Frankly, most of our interests are mundane to almost everyone but us.

Since we live in a world where we can be easily plugged-in and entertained, are we now at the point where we expect to be entertained with everything we do? Certainly we have moved far beyond the days of our grandparents, who told us they could entertain themselves with a stick and rock. Maybe this shift from our grandparents' way of life is not morally neutral. Although having options is great, possibly our belief that we have a right to be entertained is misshaping us. This is especially so since we are still "who we are" because of the mundane things we do. Our meals keep us healthy, and yet we would never skip a meal because it was boring. Our friends and family can be boring, and yet we would never deprive ourselves of their company.

And so, perhaps we would benefit by returning to a sacramental emphasis in worship, asking, What if we changed from seeing the sacraments as us interacting with them to imagining what God is doing to us through them? This would require us to review the historical meaning, usage, and purpose of the sacraments.[3]

---

3. For the sake of this book, I am speaking of the sacraments as baptism and Communion. I wish that many evangelicals and Protestants would expand what they consider to be sacraments, but the agreed upon sacraments are baptism and Communion. Let's begin recapturing a theology and practice of these first!

The Nicene Creed declares that there is one baptism. Yet we have come to a popular position that baptism is appropriate after every reconversion. This stance is both noncreedal and easily refuted. Normally, we should be baptized only once in our lives, because baptism is more about God's activity in saving humanity and not about our individual wills. We are simply responding to what God is doing in the world. And so, if we stray in life, we do not need to be rebaptized, because God has not moved; he has remained the same, steadfast and true to the same covenant as when we came to the baptismal font months or years before. God has remained faithful through it all; we are the ones who strayed. Perhaps there is a better way to say "I am back!" than revisiting a sacrament that is about what God is doing, not what we are doing. Paul, in 1 Corinthians 11, argues that we should examine ourselves before coming to the Table of our Lord. As such, it is the Table where baptized, repentant backsliders may come to recognize they've sinned and to receive forgiveness and absolution.

In my tradition, we began to struggle with the frequency of Communion when Methodism, our theological forebear, split from the Anglican Church in America. There were not enough ordained pastors in the newly formed Methodist Church to regularly oversee Communion in the burgeoning American churches, especially after the Revolution. Thus churches were only required, at a minimum, to celebrate Communion once every three months. The struggle was to get more ordained pastors, or elders. Itinerant ministry became the practice, with one pastor responsible for several churches. The three-month mandate was given to ensure such pastors offered this meal to all their people regularly; this ruling was not meant to be a minimum standard for churches with full-time pastors. Although helpful at the time, this necessary pragmatism has in some ways hurt the church's mission of worship. As full-time parish ministers began to apply the three-month minimum requirement to their local churches, the frequency of Communion dropped. The church thus gradually marginalized the very act that Jesus instituted and commanded us to practice.

Perhaps, then, we should recover an attitude of excitement each time we gather together and come to the Table, because Jesus himself has prepared this feast. We come to the Table, hopefully regularly, in anticipation that we get to share a meal with Jesus. When we read the Gospels, Jesus is constantly sitting down to have a meal with people. We should pay attention to Jesus's meal companions, because their identity is vitally important to the Gospel story. As we read through the table scenes, we find that Jesus is usually with people who are "unworthy," those who do not "belong." The Pharisees and the holy people are upset because they believe they are the ones worthy to sit at the table with Jesus, but instead Jesus keeps inviting tax collectors, sinners, the poor, and others who do not measure up to have a meal with him.

When we prepare the Lord's Table, pray over the elements, and read the words of institution,[4] we are inviting the actual presence of Christ—who, we testify, is alive—to come and be among us. Roman Catholics talk about transubstantiation; they believe that when they pray over the meal, it becomes the actual body and blood of Christ. This is not the Protestant belief. What we do believe in the Protestant tradition is that when we open the Table, read the words of institution, and pray the epiclesis,[5] the presence

---

[4]. Often, I will simply read I Corinthians 11:23-26, or an expanded version, with compelling verses before and after.

[5]. This word is from *epiklēsis*, Greek for "invocation" or "calling down from on high." This is a prayer where the celebrant invokes the Holy Spirit upon the bread and wine.

of Christ by the Spirit comes to dwell among us, that spiritually Christ is giving his body and blood[6] once again to us.

There is a saying that you are what you eat. It means that eating healthy foods will make a person healthy and that eating unhealthy foods will make a person unhealthy. But what if, when we come to the Table, we apply that statement afresh, and say, "I am what I eat, and what I eat today is the body and blood of Christ." The real presence of Christ is present spiritually at the Table, and Christ gives himself to us to dwell within us.

Matt Maher wrote a worship song that I love to sing, "Lord, I Need You." There is a line in that song I love; it says, "Holiness is Christ in me."[7] If this is true, that holiness, or sanctification, is Christ "in me," Communion is the meal of sanctification. Upon giving our lives to Christ and believing that he saves us, cleanses us, and removes sin from our lives, we come to this Table, and as we partake of the body and blood of Christ by the Spirit through the bread and the cup, we take in Christ. We are what we eat! This meal of sanctification is the spiritual reception of his body and blood into our body through physical means so that Christ becomes part of us. Christ, in our baptism, consumes us into his body, and at the Table we consume his body into ours.

If we want to be a sanctified, holy people, we would do well to come to the body and blood of Christ and invite his presence into our bodies, reminding us that it is only through Christ that we can possibly become holy. We cannot work harder; we cannot imagine

---

6. "The Lord's Supper is a means of grace in which Christ is present by the Spirit." "The Lord's Supper," Article XIII, in *Manual/2017–2021: Church of the Nazarene* (Kansas City: Nazarene Publishing House, 2017), para. 13.

7. Matt Maher, vocalist, "Lord, I Need You," by Christy Nockels, Daniel Carson, Jesse Reeves, Kristian Stanfill, Matt Maher, released 2013, track 4 on *All the People Said Amen*, Essential Records 83061-0968-2, 2013, compact disc.

ourselves better and then work toward our goal. We only become holy through the grace of God, and we become holy by receiving that grace. The Table is perhaps the best place for us to do that.

Another figure of speech we use in our society today is that of bad blood. People say, "I've got bad blood with him," or "They've got bad blood between each other." Sporting teams that have deep-seated rivalries have bad blood: Alabama and Auburn, Yankees and Red Sox, and so on.

Bad blood holds grudges, wishes ill on the other, can explode at any moment. Yet when we talk about Communion, we talk about good blood—blood that restores, renews, and fixes relationships. But our society likes to talk about bad blood. They don't like good blood. News channels and clickbait websites like a good scandal. People like it whenever there is anger between friends. People like to see cops fighting or shooting in the streets, and they pull out cell phones, take pictures, and post them on the Internet.

People like it when there's bad blood and get excited when they see it. And that idea has been captured in the 2014 Taylor Swift song "Bad Blood." One of the lines is, "Band-Aids don't fix bullet holes."[8] The anger, frustration, and hatred in this song are tangible. And people love songs like this! Just imagine preteen girls listening to this song and thinking about girls who have sent mean texts about them at school. People love rivalry and particularly love seeing other people stir the pot of drama. Millions of dollars are made every year on drama and the misfortunes of other people. This is especially so when someone like Taylor Swift can capture the angst and thirst for revenge that people feel. It soothes their anger ever so temporarily.

---

8. Taylor Swift, vocalist, "Bad Blood," by Taylor Swift, Max Martin, Shellback, recorded 2014, track 8 on *1989*, Big Machine Records 470 716-6, 2014, compact disc.

What is disturbing is that this song could be sung and celebrated in almost every church. Although not wanting to express such feelings openly, people sitting in the same sanctuaries of many churches have bad blood between them. And this is not a new problem! The apostle Paul wrote to a church whose members had very bad blood between them. He had to sort out how people should treat each other in the church and then how they should come to Communion. Today we owe a great debt to the dramatic church in Corinth because a theology of how Christians should come to Communion developed as a result of the dysfunction of the Corinthian church. Frustrated by the Corinthians' behavior, Paul lays out three different things they need to consider when coming to the Table. But before examining these three things, let's explore the context of the Corinthian church.

Christians did not meet in nice cathedrals or even in nice sanctuaries as they do today; they would meet weekly, often secretly, in someone's house. They would gather together and have a feast. The meal itself would be considered Communion; eating together in love and sharing with each other was a reminder of the Last Supper. They would sing, read some Scripture, have a short talk, celebrate Communion, and return to their homes.

Now in Corinth, members would meet together in their house church, but the richer members would bring more food, take more of it, and go to a separate room. The poorer members would have to scrape together what was left over and be relegated to another room. There were distinctions being made between socioeconomic classes, and the people as a whole were not eating together.

Paul, now having been away for years, was very frustrated with the Corinthian situation, because the people had missed the point of what Jesus intended when he instituted the Communion feast. He writes to them, responding out of his frustration. Although, as 1 Corinthians attests, Paul is aggravated about several issues in the Corinthian church, this matter about Communion is one of the more significant issues. He instructs them, pointing out that if they celebrate Communion as Jesus intended, a better Christian ethic would likely flow out of its practice.

It is at the Table that Paul offers a means to fix the bad blood between the people of the Corinthian church. For him, the prescription to cure the bad blood is the good blood of Jesus Christ, which forgives. The good blood doesn't keep a record of wrongs. It doesn't lob accusations and start fights. It's steady and present, and it keeps coming to us, no matter how far we have strayed. Paul says it best in his own words:

> In the following directives I have no praise for you, for your meetings do more harm than good. In the first place, I hear that when you come together as a church, there are divisions among you, and to some extent I believe it. No doubt there have to be differences among you to show which of you have God's approval. So then, when you come together, it is not the Lord's Supper you eat, for when you are eating, some of you go ahead with your own private suppers. As a result, one person remains hungry and another gets drunk. Don't you have homes to eat and drink in? Or do you despise the church of God by humiliating those who have nothing? What shall I say to you? Shall I praise you? Certainly not in this matter!
>
> For I received from the Lord what I also passed on to you: The Lord Jesus, on the night he was betrayed, took bread, and when he had given thanks, he broke it and said, "This is my body, which is for you; do this in remembrance of me." In the same way, after supper he took the cup, saying, "This cup is the new covenant in my blood; do this, whenever you drink it,

in remembrance of me." For whenever you eat this bread and drink this cup, you proclaim the Lord's death until he comes.

So then, whoever eats the bread or drinks the cup of the Lord in an unworthy manner will be guilty of sinning against the body and blood of the Lord. Everyone ought to examine themselves before they eat of the bread and drink from the cup. For those who eat and drink without discerning the body of Christ eat and drink judgment on themselves. That is why many among you are weak and sick, and a number of you have fallen asleep. But if we were more discerning with regard to ourselves, we would not come under such judgment. Nevertheless, when we are judged in this way by the Lord, we are being disciplined so that we will not be finally condemned with the world.

So then, my brothers and sisters, when you gather to eat, you should all eat together. Anyone who is hungry should eat something at home, so that when you meet together it may not result in judgment. (1 Cor. 11:17-34)

There are three basic divisions and instructions that are happening in this text, in this community. First, the Lord's Table must express the community's unity as the new-covenant people of God. God called the people of Israel out of Egypt, away from slavery, and to the promised land. Jesus, in the Last Supper, is celebrating the immediate impetus for that exodus, the Passover. And so, God didn't call just some of the people of Israel, the ones who seemed most important to him, but rather, he called the entire community, the whole nation: the good, the bad, the frustrating, the good-looking, the rich, and the poor. He gathered them, delivered them from slavery, and led them to the promised land. And so it is likewise when we share this meal. It is an expression of our being the new-covenant people of God. We should be keenly aware of who our Communion companions are to ensure we are in unity with them. We should be praying for the perfecting work of the grace of God on those we join in Communion. We are invited to this meal to recall the deep love of God for us and to imagine how it is we can love and express our love toward those around us.

Second, Paul writes that the Lord's Supper draws attention to the church's remembrance of Jesus and his death. In 1 Corinthians 11, the Greek word for "remembrance" (vv. 24-25) carries the sense that we are calling Jesus back; the word implies more than mere mental memory and hints at Christ's presence in the feast. Not only is Jesus present during Communion, but also by participating in Communion, we "proclaim the Lord's death until he comes" (v. 26). We proclaim that the Lord Jesus Christ died on our behalf, that he bled and suffered, and that he will come again in his fullness. Calling Christ back to us in Communion both in the sense of his presence and in the sense our memory of his life and actions becomes formative and instructive to us as we worship at the Table. Moreover, the words of institution and the partaking of Communion are missional, for through them we proclaim the good news of Jesus and the hope of his return.

And finally, Communion is an occasion for us to ponder God's judgment. Often when we think of God's judgment, we feel apprehensive. But instead of feeling apprehensive, we can be thankful[9] for the grace that makes the difference between how far we can make it on our own and where God is inviting us to be. As we partake of the bread and the cup, we recall just how powerful the grace of God is—that it is shaping us to be like Christ and that we cannot by ourselves become more Christlike. Instead, we con-

---

9. The word "Eucharist," another word for Communion, comes from the Greek word *eucharistos*, which simply means "thankful." Communion, or the Eucharist, is an act of thanksgiving.

tinue to come to the broken and wounded body of Christ, receive it, and find that the more of Christ we receive—that is, the more we deepen our relationship with Christ through this sacrament and other means of grace—the more he shapes and forms us to be holy. As Christ's love fills us, we find it expelling our desire to sin. That is the work of grace in our lives. The sacrament of Communion is the sacrament of sanctification.

I love the movie *Field of Dreams* because I love baseball. In the movie, a farmer, Ray (Kevin Costner), hears a voice saying, "If you build it, he will come."[10] So Ray begins building a baseball diamond in his Iowa cornfield. No one lives near him, so it is a nonsensical call upon his life. He does not understand why he is supposed to build a baseball diamond in his backyard, but he plows out the corn, lays sod, and creates the diamond. And eventually, legends such as Shoeless Joe Jackson, who has long been dead, emerge from the outfield corn crops.

At long last, Shoeless Joe, the player disgraced by accusations that he threw a world series in 1919, has a place to play ball. He begins to bring other deceased ball-playing legends, and they play epic games in the Iowa cornfield.

Eventually, Ray's brother, who has been cynical the whole movie, sees the baseball players play and is predictably amazed at the possibilities. Suddenly he becomes supportive. A final game is played, and among the players, Ray sees his father. He is flabbergasted to see his dad as a young man. And he asks his wife, "What should I do?" And his wife says, "Well, I don't know. Introduce him to his granddaughter." Ray introduces his father to the girl, and they have an awkward exchange. Ray is excited and unsure

---

10. *Field of Dreams*, directed by Phil Alden Robinson (1989; Los Angeles: Universal Studios Home Entertainment, 2019), Blu-ray.

whether his dad recognizes him. So they talk, and as his dad turns to walk away, Ray invites his dad to play catch. It is a moving moment to all.

Ray's dad asks Ray if this is heaven.

There is something beautiful about that moment that can help us here. Father and son get lost in the delight of being with each other, of seeing each other in ways that were unexpected. Neither can decipher whether this is Iowa or heaven. They cannot distinguish between what is earthly and what is the delight of the world to come.

This is what coming to the Table should be like for us as we respond to the call of the worship service. By this point, the service should have reminded us of the grace of God found in Christ, who has died, been resurrected, has ascended to heaven, and is preparing a banquet table to dine and celebrate with us in his new creation. And when we come to the Table, we get a foretaste of that final heavenly banquet. We experience a moment when heaven crashes into earth, when we no longer know if we are in the present world or the one that is to come. As we come to the Table and receive the gift of his body and blood, we begin to wonder, "Am I in my local church, or am I in heaven?"

The answer to both parts of that question should be, hopefully, yes. On the one hand, we are in this world as God's creation, and that is good. On the other hand, heaven has broken into our very sanctuary, and the presence of God has come in a mysterious way, into the bread and the cup through the work of the Holy Spirit, and we taste just a little of what heaven will be like. In this moment, the grace and presence of God rushes over us, like a wild, flowing river, and we sense the presence of Christ, and we say, "It's not about me; it's about you. And you change me into something incredible because you are so incredible."

This moment of response is incredible, mysterious, emotional, confusing, exciting, and magnificent; it is heaven crashing into earth and losing us in the glory of God. It is not only tangible and mundane but also mysterious and spiritual. This is the essence of sacrament.

Communion may not seem meaningful this time, but it may be next time. And every time, it's Christ's invitation for us to come and receive his gift. It's an invitation for us to go out changed, because we have come into contact with the living, breathing, resurrected Lord. And that cannot but help affect the kind of people we are becoming by grace. We are shaped through the liturgy to be a people who receive the grace and presence of God.

12
Benediction

• • •

I grew up in a classic evangelical, conservative Christian family in the 1980s and 1990s. If we listened, as a family, to "secular music," it was usually the oldies from the 1950s and 1960s: Buddy Holly, Elvis Presley, the Beach Boys, the Beatles, and so on. I was fifteen when I first held my breath and snuck a "secular" CD into my house, hoping that my mom would not see it. It was the silky vocals of Rob Thomas singing for the debut album of Matchbox 20, *Yourself or Someone like You*. This was the way I was raised.

One artist I was aware of was Frank Sinatra, but I didn't know any of his songs. My family didn't listen to Sinatra because my parents were put off by his lifestyle. When I was a teenager, my pastor lambasted a Frank Sinatra song during his sermon. It was one of Sinatra's best-known songs: "My Way." The pastor talked about how wrong that song was and how no one should live that way! I had never heard the song before, so I went home and looked it up and discovered I loved it. I couldn't think of a better way to go about living life! I was not supposed to feel that way, but the song felt nearly like a personal anthem. So I got it on CD and played it regularly. I wanted to—and did—do it my way, just like the Chairman of the Board!

As I grew older and drew nearer to God, I began to understand what that pastor was saying. The holy life is lived in submission to God, not at the pleasure of our will. We are to be a people of submission, not a people conquering the world and living life "my way." Instead of living "my way," we should imagine ourselves living Jesus's way. Jesus says, "Seek ye first the kingdom of God, and his righteousness; and all these things shall be added unto you" (Matt. 6:33, KJV).

When I was a child, my mother used to sing to me the well-known song that puts that entire verse to music.[1] So I have heard "Seek ye first the kingdom of God" all my life, and yet I struggled to balance "my way" with seeking first the kingdom. I was in a passionate intellectual and existential pursuit of doing both. It took decades to realize that seeking first the kingdom of God is the opposite of trying to build my kingdom "my way." It is impossible to do both at the same time.

I've tried to demonstrate throughout this book that sometimes subconsciously, we find ourselves participating in alternative kingdoms that are not the kingdom of God. We go to church on Sunday (and maybe also on Wednesday night), but then we are bombarded for many hours the rest of the week with images, opportunities, sounds, and tastes that may be benign but may also be inviting us to participate in kingdoms that are alternatives to Christ's kingdom.

---

1. See Karen Lafferty, "Seek Ye First" (© 1972 Maranatha! Music), in *Sing to the Lord* (Kansas City: Lillenas, 1993), no. 90.

Kingdoms that ask for our allegiance and passion that are not the kingdom of God are idols of this world. Let us be careful to consider where we direct our love.

Between worship services, experiences and phenomena happen that are formational; they can build and form us into a particular kind of person. Such experiences can include a song on the radio, a blockbuster movie, a new iPhone, news of an upcoming political battle, and a sale at the mall. The *National Enquirer* can make us voyeurs of the rich and famous, when all we want to do is purchase a gallon of milk. A dinner party can make us less appreciative of what we have and jealous of what our neighbors have. And Christmas can become about hustle and bustle and presents instead of worship.

These experiences tend to encourage anger, vengeance, jealousy, hatred, and consumerism. Consider how far those traits are from the fruit of the Spirit: "love, joy, peace, patience, kindness, goodness, faithfulness, gentleness, [and] self-control" (Gal. 5:22-23, ESV). The banal things of our society quietly creep up within us, leaving us with attitudes that are un-Christlike. We get caught up in these things in our lives, and they are creating us to be a certain kind of person—an un-Christlike person.

Consider John 13 as an example of who Christ is and what Christ does. Jesus is praying that his disciples would be known by their love: "By this everyone will know that you are my disciples, if you love one another" (v. 35). Go out on the streets today and ask passersby what they think of Christians—and mark down how many of them say, "They're the most loving bunch in the city." The total is not likely to be high. Instead, we are known for our bullhorns.

We are known for creating boxes that people must fit in, for loving the law, and for being suspicious of grace. We are known for placing barriers between people and God. As people of Scripture, it is embarrassing how far we often are from the simple call of Christ. We have become something different from the people Christ invites us to be in the world.

In a world with competing liturgies, it not surprising that we are a confused bunch. We find and make meaning in so many places, and worship is receiving less and less of our time.

The simple flow of Christian liturgy can vary, but it often involves gathering, singing, greeting, reading Scripture, praying, receiving offerings, proclaiming the gospel, responding, and, finally, giving and receiving the benediction. The benediction is a vital part of worship. It is a blessing given from pastor to people, asking God to empower them with his Spirit to go and embody the narrative of the worship service as they inhabit the world. We are called to live out the good news in the world, and we are inviting the liturgy we have just experienced to shape us in a way that would help us remain steadfastly loyal to God in a liturgical world. The worship service is never simply an hour we put on our calendars to give back to God because he is good to us. Worship is when we are breathed into God's presence so that God can gather us up into himself as a worshipping community and then breathe us back out to practice what we have seen and heard in his presence.[2]

When we gather to worship, God exposes his presence; he descends on and among us. The etymology of the word "doxology" is helpful here. It is the combination of two Greek words *doxa*, which means "glory," and *logia*, which means "saying." Doxologies are "sayings of glory." A doxology is a two-way movement; the glory of God descends on the people, and the people respond by lifting

---

2. See Brent D. Peterson, *Created to Worship: God's Invitation to Become Fully Human* (Kansas City: Beacon Hill Press of Kansas City, 2012), 41-44.

up their praises. It is a mysterious moment in which God's presence breaks in and we give our praise back to God. Heaven and earth meet in the middle. This doxological happening should be the impetus for our Christian life. We should open ourselves, with intention, to be formed by our liturgical participation in doxology. The benediction is the moment when we are invited to receive a blessing that reminds us of that doxological moment and calls us to embody it as we leave the church. The gathered body scatters with a call to bear the glory of God that inhabited this space out to the world for the sake of the world.

Worship, then, invites us to be "glory bearers," or those who have come so close to the glory of God that it imprints itself on us as we go. The glory of God is seen through us because of our incredible encounter with God. Consider the story of Moses in the Old Testament when he climbs up Mount Sinai, angry at the Israelites for building a golden calf while he was receiving the commandments of God. On returning to the top, Moses asks God, in light of the difficult people and the journey ahead of him, to "show me your glory" (Exod. 33:18). God warns, "No one may see me and live" (v. 20).

How great a God is this? The presence of God is so heavy that we as humans can't even handle it in its fullness. But God grants Moses's yearning for his glory in part, saying, "There is a place near me where you may stand on a rock. When my glory passes by, I will put you in a cleft in the rock and cover you with my hand until I have passed by. Then I will remove my hand and you will see my back; but my face must not be seen" (vv. 21-23).

Moses experiences this because he pleads with God to give him guidance and power to lead a sinful, stiff-necked people on the treacherous journey they were undertaking. Standing in the glory of God is not to receive a spiritual high; it is a gift for the journey and strength for the call. We are missing the point if we receive the glory of God as a gift and then hoard it. We must go, changed by the experience, charged with mission.

And when Moses sees the glory of God, his face glows in such a way that when he climbs down the mountain, the Israelites who are at its foot see Moses and know that he has changed. It's not just that there's something in his heart that's a little different. They see in his face that something has changed, and they want to know what has happened. The presence of God was so real to him that people could see a difference.

Now imagine if we catch a vision like this in our worship! What if when we come to worship on Sunday morning, we expect the glory of God to come among us and grab hold of us as we leave the sanctuary? What if we then also expect that on Monday morning, people in our offices, in our schools, or in whatever places we go will think, "There's just something a little different about that Christian." And when they ask, "What is happening with you?" the answer will be, "I've been in the presence of almighty God this weekend. And I plan to be in the presence of God again next weekend."

Hopefully, when we begin to orient our lives around a pattern that begins and ends with us longing to be in the presence of God, our worship time will begin to color who we are the rest of the week. That is, when we go to the mall or watch a movie, we will begin to see metaphors of who God is, we will begin to see the presence of Christ, and we will begin to see the face of God on people. No longer will our experiences between our times of worship be the forces creating who we are to be. No longer will we hear a song and allow it to shape our worldview. Christ, who has encountered us in profound ways, will now help us interpret the world we live in. Encountering Christ changes the entire narrative.

Being a Christian in our world today is not always a full expression of what the Scriptures envision. Although we may consider the Sermon on the Mount as the primary ethic for Christians, we often find in the United States Christians who overly emphasize and love the law. Wars are even waged over whether American courtrooms should hang copies of the Ten Commandments on their walls. But are Christians actually following the Ten Commandments?

When I was a child, church discipleship programs encouraged me to memorize the Ten Commandments. As I memorized the words, I began to analyze what they mean. I would begin with, "You shall not murder" (Exod. 20:13). I always began there because I was confident I could keep it. I was less sure about, "Honor your father and your mother" (v. 12). I also was not confident about, "You shall not covet your neighbor's house . . . neighbor's [spouse] . . . or anything that belongs to your neighbor" (v. 17). Frankly, I was always really upset that my mom would not let me have a video game system when all my friends did. Coveting was pretty close to home for me, so I did not want to talk or think about that one.

The first few commandments didn't really bother me; they seemed doable:

You shall have no other gods before me. (V. 3)

All right, God is number one. Check!

You shall not make for yourself an image in the form of anything in heaven above or on the earth beneath or in the waters below. You shall not bow down to them or worship them; for I, the LORD your God, am a jealous God, punishing the children for the sin of the parents to the third and fourth generation of those who hate me, but showing love to a thousand generations of those who love me and keep my commandments. (Vv. 4-6)

Okay, check! There's a story about a golden calf in Exodus. I'll never find gold and boil it into a calf.

> You shall not misuse the name of the LORD your God, for the LORD will not hold anyone guiltless who misuses his name. (V. 7).

All right, so I decided anytime I said "Jesus Christ," it would not be immediately after hitting my hand with a hammer; it would only be in church when I was talking about the incarnate God himself. Check!

> Remember the Sabbath day by keeping it holy. Six days you shall labor and do all your work, but the seventh day is a sabbath to the LORD your God. On it you shall not do any work, neither you, nor your son or daughter, nor your male or female servant, nor your animals, nor any foreigner residing in your towns. For in six days the LORD made the heavens and the earth, the sea, and all that is in them, but he rested on the seventh day. Therefore the LORD blessed the Sabbath day and made it holy. (Vv. 8-11)

My family went to church every single Sunday. Check!

These are the lessons the church was pouring into me; they encompassed what we were supposed to be. As I got older, I learned there was more to the law than a holy checklist. For example, the law is not a list of dos and don'ts to make people appear holy but a lifestyle that separates out the people of God to protect them from the dangers and snares of this world. The law is not about what we do or do not do but about helping us to be something. The law is meant to be a gift from God.

When the law states "You shall have no other gods before me" (Exod. 20:3), maybe what it really means is similar to those words Jesus spoke: "Seek ye first the kingdom of God, and his righteousness; and all these things shall be added unto you" (Matt. 6:33, KJV).

Seeking the kingdom first sounds good, but is God really the One our lives are wrapped around? Is he why our schedules exist, with everything flowing out of our mission to be glory bearers in a fallen world? Is God why we work the way or where we do? Is God why we spend our time and money and use our resources and efforts the way we do?

Is God really first or, in spite of the second commandment urging that we not be idolatrous, have we constructed idols not made of gold but built from what we truly love? Can "success" be an idol? Have we made getting a scholarship for our child an idol? Have we made financial comforts our idol? Have we made getting a bigger house in a better neighborhood our idol? Idols are not always simple golden packages that we kneel down and meditate before. An idol is anything or anyone that we give ourselves more fully to than we do to God. Idols are anything we need in addition to Jesus to be happy.

"You shall not misuse the name of the LORD your God" (Exod. 20:7). We are trained to say pleasant things when we hit our thumb with the hammer, so is that enough? When we read this and think about it, this commandment is not just saying, "Do not use the name of God as a swear word." Although this misuse is certainly encompassed by this commandment, something much deeper than swearing is intended. The commandment is getting at the heart of how we live; it is telling us not to misuse the name of the Lord our God by claiming to be members of his people—Christians—and then living as if that does not matter. That would be a profound misuse of the name of Christ. If our testimony is that we are trying to be like Christ, little Christs, we are telling an unbelieving world that this is what Jesus is like. If we testify with sinful behaviors, we are taking the Lord's name—Christ(ian)—in vain. If our life is proclaiming an embodied testimony that is fundamentally different from what our words are saying, we are dishonoring the name of God. When we claim to be God's children, our lives must match up with the One we claim to serve. If not, we are taking his name in vain and bearing false witness about who God is and what he is like to the world.

The final "easy command" I want to consider is to "Remember the Sabbath day by keeping it holy" (v. 8). When I was growing up, that meant, "Go to church on Sunday." But yet that only begins to scratch the surface. It's really a story of relaxing and delighting. Here, when we are talking about Sabbath, we are not simply talking about carving out an hour and a half on a Sunday morning. It's about patterning our lives after God. The God who, from the beginning, models rest. God took six days to create, and then he rested on the seventh. If God can rest, maybe we can too. And if there is any modern cultural liturgy that counter-forms us from the human beings God yearns for us to be, if there is any idol that we have completely fallen in love with and at whose altar we worship in America today, it is busyness! That is, in my estimation, our favorite god in America.

Often when we ask people, "How are you doing?" we get the answer, "Busy." Not only do people with jobs and children give this answer, but also retirees respond similarly. Instead of resting for the last twenty or so years of their lives, many seniors are going everywhere all the time, chasing grandchildren, volunteering at civic clubs, and so on. The most perplexing message from many retirees is that they just want to go back to work because it was less busy then.

We *love* busyness. And here, God is inviting us to work hard, to be busy for six days, to be productive, to make a life for ourselves! But on the seventh day, God asks us to take a moment to delight in the creation that he has given to us. We are invited to delight in God, to worship, and to rest.

Our losing sight of the profound meaning of the Ten Commandments has not served us well. Because we are struggling for our identity in this world, we get involved with things like plastering civic courts with copies of these commandments. Yet we seem to take little time to reflect on what these commandments even meant or mean. We spend more time superficially implementing them than subjecting ourselves to their deeper meaning. We yearn for hard righteousness, but we do not take the time within our busy lives to be intentionally formed by grace.

As Christians today, we are faced with sources that are not God telling us who we are supposed to be. And when we hear God telling us who we are to be, we want to say, "That's nonsense! Good luck living like that! Times are different. We can't live that way today!" We often do not hear the story of God well anymore. And we want to squeeze as much of our Christian faith as we can into our lives instead of praying, "Who am I to be, God?" Christians seem to be more uncomfortable about living life as "resident aliens," as 1 Peter puts it (2:11, EXB)[3]—that is, being in the world but not of it (see John 17:14-18). Living "of the world" (vv. 14, 16) does not differentiate Christians from secular life. But many times that is the way Christians today live; their Christian practices blend in so well with the secular lifestyle that they do not look much different from their secular friends.

That has been a fundamental theme throughout this book—that as Christians, we too often buy into the songs we hear, the

---

3. Stanley M. Hauerwas and William H. Willimon also wrote a helpful book on being resident aliens: *Resident Aliens: Life in the Christian Colony* (Nashville: Abingdon Press, 1989).

places we are supposed to go, the things we are supposed to do, the items we are supposed to buy, and so on. We have so many mediums now speaking into our lives. A hundred years ago, pastors were usually the ones who advised people on how life should be lived. Now we have radio shows, news outlets, social media, and other sources that offer their ideas of who we should be. The voices get confusing, and usually, the final product is less than the image of God.

So how do we recast our lives in light of all this? The Christian church in the West is struggling: pastors are not always adequately trained, churches are closing because they lack financial viability, and pastors are often overtaxed with ministry and secular jobs. The question we must ask is, Are we even concerned about this? American cultural liturgies encourage us to believe as long as we are fat, happy, healthy, and wealthy, we are fine. If the stock market is up, so are our spirits!

So where do we go from here? We live in a world that loves a reboot. When I was a kid, sequels came out all the time. Everyone who loved a movie, including me, would look forward to the sequel. We loved *Back to the Future*, so we wanted *Back to the Future Part II*. We were lucky enough to get *Back to the Future Part III*, and we didn't even ask for it! We loved *Home Alone*, and we got a sequel. The same robbers from the original were back again trying to harm Kevin in another booby-trapped house—this time in New York!

Sequels have lost their luster, though. Nowadays people will groan when a sequel is announced. Instead we want reboots from Hollywood. We want something new and fresh, so we get a new take on Batman or a reboot of the Spiderman series every several months. *Ghostbusters*, a great movie of the 1980s, was remade with women as the protagonists. James Bond existed through the Cold

War, and when the Cold War ended, we rebooted him! We love a reboot; we love for a story to continue, especially when it really grasps our lives and our imaginations.

Hopefully, we have connected with the Christian story in the same way. In a reboot world, a story reliant on resurrection is relevant. Therefore, we should depart from a worship service in a way that demonstrates we have interacted doxologically with the grace of God—that we have been reminded of the bad news of the world and have heard that the grace of God is good and is rebooting us, the church, again. We need a weekly reboot when we come into the presence of God to remind us who we are, whose we are, and how we should live now. My favorite way to invite the church to reboot is through benediction.

Benediction is Latin for "good word." When the liturgical work of the church is finished—we've sung, we've heard a sermon, we've had a response, we have greeted one another in peace, and so on—we now welcome a final word of benediction. We hear a benediction at the end so that no matter what we have heard, no matter what has convicted us, no matter what act has been hard, we hear a final good word that sends us out. It's the final act of us having been "breathed in by God," and this moment is when God "exhales us" back into the world.

The Epistles of the New Testament—many written by Paul—end their letters with a benediction, a good word, a reminder of who God is and who God will be in your life. A personal favorite is 2 Corinthians 13:11-14. Hear how enlivening these words are:

> Finally, brothers and sisters, rejoice! Strive for full restoration, encourage one another, be of one mind, live in peace. And the God of love and peace will be with you.
>
> Greet one another with a holy kiss. All God's people here send their greetings.

> May the grace of the Lord Jesus Christ, and the love of God, and the fellowship of the Holy Spirit be with you all.

The words here are good, not because they are easy words, especially when they begin with, "Strive for full restoration." What an exhortation! The idea is put things in order with God, each other, and Paul. But we are reminded in hard callings that it is the God of love who will accompany us and help us. He loves us and is working for the church. Not only do we have God's work, but also we are gifted with a community of saints. The Christian life is lived in communal encouragement. We, the church, can do this together! We also see that "the grace of the Lord Jesus Christ, and the love of God, and the fellowship of the Holy Spirit"—the triune God—will "be with you" as you "strive for full restoration" and hear the appeal of the author. This is good news, a beautiful charge, and meant to fill our cups as we leave the sanctuary of praise but not the presence of God. God has offered to go with us as we bear the name of Christ.

Another great scriptural benediction is 2 Thessalonians 3:16-18:

> Now may the Lord of peace himself give you peace at all times and in every way. The Lord be with all of you.
>
> I, Paul, write this greeting in my own hand, which is the distinguishing mark in all my letters. This is how I write.
>
> The grace of our Lord Jesus Christ be with you all.

Imagine the pastor, in this case the apostle Paul, wishing nothing more in your life but that there would be genuine peace in everything that you do. How we receive those good words can fill us with hope as we go.

The blessing and the benediction, in so many ways, are the marching orders by which we are, by God, exhaled back into the world. Now that we have been doxologically engaged with God, now that we have been grafted in and brought into God's presence, God sends us out to be his people in the world he loves. These are the marching orders that we're given, to be his people, lost in his grace, with a task given to us by the sermon and the Scripture of that day; we are to be something on his behalf, until he invites us back into his presence, corporately, and next Sunday breathes us back in and gives us a taste of his heaven to send us back out again. It's an important moment in our worship service.

The Lord of the Rings trilogy, by J. R. R. Tolkien, is preceded by a book called *The Hobbit*. They are separate stories but connected. Bilbo writes the tale, and Frodo continues it from his experiences and perspective. At the end of the third part of the trilogy, *The Return of the King*, in the film version, when Frodo is shown writing the end of his story, Sam, a friend, comes in and sees this and exclaims, "You finished it!" There is tangible excitement that the story has been written.

Frodo recognized that while the part of the story he is telling has come to a conclusion, the story is not complete. So at the end of the movie Frodo hands the completed book to Sam and tells him, "There is room for a little more."

We have received a compelling story in our Holy Scriptures. We have been gifted the story of God's redemption for the world, a story of grace and love, benevolence and care. The benediction is a moment like the conclusion of *The Lord of the Rings*, when we as worshippers are given the story of God and told, "Keep writing!" Now the biblical canon is closed, but the story of God is still being written, and it is being written by us, God's people.

We live in a world with many competing narratives and images of the good life. There are so many things trying to grasp our hearts and imaginations and invite us to be this way or do this thing. But the Christian narrative, reenacted week after week in liturgical worship, should be the story that is ultimately grabbing our hearts and shaping our lives. It is in worship, gathered in the presence of God, that we are most strongly formed to be the kind of people God is calling us to be. It is imperative that we gather week in and week out to be breathed into the presence of God.

Finally, at the culmination of worship, the benediction is pronounced, and we are sent forth. We are invited at this moment to be the people of God, on mission, as we go into the world. The call pronounced is to keep writing the story of God with our lives, through the grace God has given us. We are invited to be his glory bearers, having been in the presence of his glory.

Let's go and write the story of God before all whom we meet. And while we are writing the story, let's allow that story, the story of God's redemption, to be what is primarily causing us to be who we are. Let's not allow the noise of the rest of the world to wrestle us away from the grace of God.

Afterword

• • •

A child is born in the United States of America: "It's a girl!" She is born into a middle-class family that immediately adorns her with designer clothes with cute sayings about who her aunt is or what her sister thinks of her birth. Mom and Dad, adept in the culture, keep their daughter at home except for doctor's appointments. The world is chaotic, and this child will be kept safe.

After a few months have passed, it occurs to Mom that the child should be brought to church. Mom's Catholic grandmother used to say something about baptizing the child in case something horrific happened so that the child would not be damned to hell. Mom does not believe this, but it seems important to make sure that their darling daughter is not in danger.

The parents present the child to the pastor of the church they have attended off and on since their marriage and ask what the next step is. They are Christians, because they believe in Jesus. The pastor asks if they would like to dedicate or baptize this child. Stunned that there are options, the parents ask about the implications of each. Being open-minded, progressive parents, they decide they want the child to make a personal decision about following

Jesus, but because they believe in God, they will dedicate the child in a church they themselves are marginally dedicated to. That is the safest route.

After the dedication, the parents increase their attendance. They make sure their child goes to Sunday school, and they are in church every Sunday they are free. This works well for five years. At that point, their daughter begins playing sports, enrolls in dance class, and is a Daisy Scout. Soccer, would you believe it, now uses Sunday morning as part of its schedule. It should be okay, because it only lasts eight weeks. Dance class is on Wednesday nights, but their daughter really wants to go, plus all of her kindergarten friends are there. As a result, attendance in midweek discipleship activities begins to dry up as well.

The next year, the child begins first grade. In class, she learns the Pledge of Allegiance and hears the national anthem every day. She is taught the history of the nation and civic allegiance. At home, when the family watches football on Sunday afternoons, there is much discussion on the television about standing for the anthem.

It is becoming clear that the house Mom and Dad bought years before she was born is now going to be too small with a younger brother coming along. So the family moves out to the suburbs to a gorgeous house that is mortgaged to the furthest extent of the family budget. More space, newer appliances, and an open concept are exactly what this family needs to function well. They leave their church behind, especially since they will now be commuting farther to work all week. This is okay, because they will find a new church in their new neighborhood.

As the child grows, there is increasing pressure to dress the part of the suburban school. Frequent trips to the mall ensue. At the mall, there are stores adorned with advertising images that sell people, not on a shirt or pair of pants, but on a better life: thinner, fairer, better dressed, happier. The daughter picks up on this and develops her own style. What Mom picks out is no longer good enough; the daughter needs to decide on it herself.

Soccer is going great. In the new suburb, she has found a traveling club that occupies three nights a week and every other weekend. She is making new friends, developing her game, and piling up trophies and acclaim. People are even beginning to wonder if a college scholarship is in her future. She is ten.

During these suburban years, Mom and Dad find a church that they can call home, but they cannot get plugged in well. They are only in town one or two weekends a month. The church is a bit larger than they are used to, so it is hard to navigate the bulletin and know where to go next. Their promotions have made work difficult, and frankly, they are often tired at the end of the week—and that is before factoring in caring for two children, both with their own lives. Not only that, but they find church to be just a little boring. It is the same thing every week: singing, awkward greeting times, asking for money, preacher getting up and talking. Although this church is filled with decent people, it just doesn't seem to connect with them. They do their best to drop some money in an offering plate here and there and maybe serve at the soup kitchen if it fits their schedule, but connecting with the church's activities is difficult with their busy lifestyle.

The more challenging church attendance becomes, with their packed schedule, the more Mom listens to podcasted sermons. It's not fellowship, but at least it is the "word," and the preaching is better than that at the local church. Unconsciously and subconsciously, they begin to view the world and its activities, not from the perspective of the church, but from the viewpoint of the twenty-four-hour news. The politics of the news network is the same as they thought the church's was, so they assume the message is the same.

High school begins, and with it come iPhones, Abercrombie and Fitch, varsity roster spots, homework, chess club, high school musicals, first chair in the band, Twitter, a summer job, car insurance, boyfriends, social engagements, Snapchat, college applications, class trips to DC, and a Spanish class spring break to Mexico. All these things are the expected activities of red-blooded American teens, so they are uncritically linked together. It's just common sense; it's what they are expected to do. It is "how you get into a good college."

College begins, and church does not matter for the usual reasons: early wake-up times, boring preachers, only day to just relax, wanting to be spiritual but not religious, too old-fashioned, doesn't get modern times.

Meanwhile, all of the values of the daughter's childhood have become firmly rooted: patriotism, sports, consumerism, economics, relaxation, technology, travel, and security. These virtues are all formed by a liturgical life. She was subjected to patterns of this world that seem amoral. While the church was busy protecting itself from swear words, alcohol, and other issues, it missed that the worship of God was being usurped by the worship of the tamer parts of culture.

This fable is a story all too familiar to those of us who have been in the church for many years. We are seeing new generations decide they do not need church, sometimes even rejecting God. In response to this, the church often tries to keep up with the culture, mirroring what is considered cool or hip. These efforts so often result from the question *what*. What do people want? What are people doing instead of going to church? What will attract people back? We are so far down the road of *what* that questions of *why* often bring angry looks or blank stares. If we are honest, church leaders would more likely answer *why* with, "Because we have always done it this way."

I heard a story about a church that welcomed a new pastor to what she thought was a strange ritual. They would all sit close to each other toward the front, and then following her pastoral prayer, they would disperse across the sanctuary to their preferred seats. She decided to ask her lay leaders why.

No one could answer.

One lady said that her grandmother, who was in hospice, may remember the origin. She went to her grandmother's room and asked why the church did this. Grandmother smiled and said that before they were able to afford central heat, they would stoke a fire in the front of the sanctuary. By the time prayer was completed, the whole of the sanctuary was sufficiently warmed, and people could return to their pews.

This book has been an extended argument for *why*. Let us, as the church, no longer look to what is cool but return to why we do what we do as a gathered liturgical, worshipping body. This may mean spending time considering ancient practices of the church that we have neglected: the passing of the peace, regular celebrations of the Eucharist, intentional public readings of the Scripture, and more. The church has two thousand years of wisdom about Christian worship. Perhaps we should turn to the history of the church, remembering *why* we do what we do. We should do this instead of turning to cultural liturgies as a normative practice for a postmodern people.

There are some who would argue that a liturgical revival would simply be rote, formal behavior. It certainly can become this if we are not careful. But then coming to church every week, singing three songs, and having a prayer, a sermon, and an altar call can be every bit as rote or formalized.

Somehow, we do not find liturgical acts such as standing for the national anthem to be boring, but we do find standing for songs at church to be so. Somehow, we are thrilled to run our credit card through restaurant and department store machines, but we are upset at writing a check to the church. Somehow, we have decided that Jesus wants us to be safe, secure, happy, and prosperous, but he took risks, was self-sacrificing, was a man of sorrows, and ministered to the poor.

Our liturgies in church matter, because the liturgies we participate in form us at a primal, internal level. Television shows, school curricula, advertisements, music, and civic activities are all arguing for us to be moralistic, consumerist, and patriotic. But church liturgies are arguing for us to be patient, simple, reliant, Spirit-driven, forgiven and forgiving, generous, kingdom-of-God-shaped people who are called to live as foreigners to the patterns of this world. Such a call is harrowing, because we need to live at a pace and in a pattern different from our neighbors. It means we must say no to things that everyone else seems to say yes to and then indulges in.

But if I may co-opt a saying of Jesus, those who indulge in this world have received their reward in full. The things of this world are not always the "big sins." Sometimes they are simply indulgences in activities that take our eyes off of Christ and form our desires for other things.

Worship at church should never be treated as an obligation. It should be—when done with care and intention—eagerly anticipated as an experience that enlivens our senses to the presence of the living Christ. Worship should cultivate our desires and longings to be kingdom oriented. If our longing is for the kingdom, our behavior, our priorities, and our dispositions will shift.

Liturgies are powerful. They are shaping us even when we are not fully aware. Let us, the people of God, return to the liturgical work of the church as our first priority so that we will desire above all else to be shaped in the image of Christ, doing the work of Christ for the sake of Christ so that the world can be saved.

Bibliography

● ● ●

Daniels, T. Scott. *Embracing Exile: Living Faithfully as God's Unique People in the World*. Kansas City: Beacon Hill Press of Kansas City, 2017.

Duhigg, Charles. *The Power of Habit: Why We Do What We Do in Life and Business*. New York: Random House Trade Paperbacks, 2014.

"Eye Contact and Social Interaction." PsyArticles.com. Accessed October 27, 2017. http://www.psyarticles.com/inter-personal/social-interaction.htm.

Gladwell, Malcolm. *Outliers: The Story of Success*. New York: Little, Brown, 2008.

Hauerwas, Stanley M., and William H. Willimon. *The Truth about God: The Ten Commandments in Christian Life*. Nashville: Abingdon Press, 1999.

Moschella, Mary Clark. *Ethnography as a Pastoral Practice: An Introduction*. Cleveland: Pilgrim Press, 2008.

Saliers, Don E. *Worship as Theology: Foretaste of Glory Divine*. Nashville: Abingdon Press, 1994.

Schmemann, Alexander. *For the Life of the World: Sacraments and Orthodoxy*. Crestwood, NY: St. Vladimir's Seminary Press, 2002.

Schrodt, Paul. "Lady Gaga Discovered How to Be Happy When She Started Saying One Word a Lot More Often." Business Insider. Last modified October 30, 2015. http://www.businessinsider.com/lady-gaga-yale-speech-2015-10.

Sinek, Simon. "Start with Why—How Great Leaders Inspire Action." *TED Talk*. Filmed September 28, 2009. YouTube video, 18:01. https://www.youtube.com/watch?v=u4ZoJKF_VuA.

Smith, James K. A. *Desiring the Kingdom: Worship, Worldview, and Cultural Formation*. Cultural Liturgies, vol. 1. Grand Rapids: Baker Academic, 2009.

Wesselmann, Eric D., Florencia D. Cardoso, Samantha Slater, and Kipling D. Williams. "To Be Looked at as Though Air: Civil Attention Matters." Psychological Science 23, no. 2 (January 2012): 166-68, https://doi.org/10.1177/0956797611427921.

Willimon, William H. *The Service of God: Christian Work and Worship*. Nashville: Abingdon Press, 1983.

www.ingramcontent.com/pod-product-compliance
Lightning Source LLC
LaVergne TN
LVHW051556080426
835510LV00020B/3010